Ban the Performance Appraisal

The importance of workplace culture in high-performing, kind and happy organisations and how to create them.

Iggy Tan CEO

Publisher:
Lofthouse One Pty Ltd
Email: iggy.tan@bigpond.net.au

Lofthouse One Pty Ltd

Ban the Performance Appraisal

In collaboration with Dr Sally Ann-Jones
Illustrations: Iggy Tan
Graphic design: Rachel Casotti (Pictograph Pty Ltd)
Publishing Consultants: Pickawoowoo Publishing Group
Photos from iStock
All proceeds of the book support Rotary International and Beyond Blue

 A catalogue record for this book is available from the National Library of Australia

SECOND EDITION
ISBN: 978-0-9945095-2-9 (paperback)
ISBN: 978-0-9945095-3-6 (ebook)

Iggy Tan BSC MBA GAICD

Iggy Tan is a highly experienced mining and chemical industry CEO with a passion for creating high-performing workplace cultures. During his career, he has worked in large multinational, medium and small size companies.

Over his 30 years' management experience, Iggy has developed techniques on how to manage people better, producing happy, dynamic and highly effective organisations. Iggy now creates these types of working cultures in the companies he builds and manages.

Iggy holds a Master of Business Administration from the University of Southern Cross, a Bachelor of Science from the University of Western Australia and is a graduate of the Australian Institute of Company Directors.

In collaboration with Dr Sally-Ann Jones

Sally-Ann's successful career as a writer has been varied: she has worked as a freelance journalist for several decades; is the author of several romance novels; gained a PhD in Creative Writing from the University of Western Australia in 2011; and currently works in media and public relations. Sally-Ann's book Stella's Sea is her debut novel for a general readership.

Dedicated to

Judy, Emma, Jayden, Georgia and Nathan

For putting up with me

Ban the Performance Appraisal

Have performance appraisals been a source of motivation and compelled you to do your job better and more efficiently? Or have you found the performance appraisal to be unfair, demotivating, frustrating or even a waste of time?

Iggy Tan CEO shares his ideas on how to create high-performing organisations and the importance of workplace culture within an organisation. This includes banning the performance appraisal, creating a "no blame" culture, and rewarding team outcomes rather than individual performances. Iggy advocates regular, flat and direct communication and getting back to basic management.

Iggy Tan's brand of "Egalitarian Management" builds compassionate, kind and happy workplaces.

Praises for Ban the Performance Appraisal

"Loved reading the book – it is terrific…"
Emeritus Professor Gary Martin, CEO Australian Institute of Management

*"For my money Iggy Tan has blown apart one of the biggest myths in management today – this book
should be compulsory leadership "101" reading!"*
Jamie Scott, CEO, Jordan Scott Consulting (Leadership)

*"We should all know that to be successful in today's business environment we need the total team to be goal orientated, motivated, successful and rewarded – not just some of the individuals –
it just takes people like Iggy to keep reminding us of this."*
Tony Sheard, Chief Financial Officer, Mineral Commodities Ltd

"Happy employees work harder, are more dedicated to the company, they need less management and are more productive – as a result the company will be an "Employer of Choice". The points raised in this compelling book go to the core of that objective…"
Simon Morten GAICD Chief Manufacturing Improvement Officer, Cristal Global

"I enjoyed reading Iggy's refreshing approach as it speaks to the basics of human nature and what we hope management is about."
Colin Slattery, Director General Department of Lands, Government of Western Australia

"Respect – this word bounces off each page; Iggy has nailed it; so take a pinch of courage, give it a go and watch your workplace flourish."
Vicki Willing, Outcomes of Life Coaching, President Rotary Matilda Bay

"It is important that CEO's write about matters often only thought of as being the domain of HR. In Iggy's words it is fundamentally about 'respect and dignity' and good feedback is – 'constant, immediate and dynamic'."
Phil de Saint Jorre, HR Management Consultant

Contents

Foreword

Emeritus Professor Gary Martin

CEO and Executive Director of Australian Institute of Management (WA)

If you are interested in rethinking your own management and leadership of others to enhance the performance of your business or organisation, you will be very interested in reading this well-crafted, informative and revealing book, which is steeped in the author's extensive experience in leading and managing organisations.

Iggy Tan's book is much more than its title would have you believe. In Ban the Performance Appraisal, Iggy Tan challenges many conventional management and leadership practices, which are often adopted in organisations, drawn from the corporate, government, not-for-profit and community sectors. He argues that many practices adopted by managers and leaders in modern organisations create employees who actively compete with each other rather than encouraging them to work as part of united, high performing teams. The competitive atmosphere created by such practices can result in a less than desirable workplace culture, siloism and a lack of productivity.

While many organisations advocate "teamwork", Iggy advocates that the management practices being adopted facilitate the exact opposite. For example, he advises that the common practice of setting objectives for individuals often motivates employees to compete with others in their teams. What is needed, he suggests, is a set of team goals through which individuals can contribute to team performance, based on their individual strengths. Similarly, Iggy proposes that the common practice of having specific job descriptions and roles does not encourage employees to go beyond their roles and support others in their team.

It is no surprise that Iggy suggests that simply setting team objectives alone will maximise organisational performance. He argues that there a number of other important practices, which ought to be adopted including transparent communication. By way of example, Iggy makes the point that the conventional practice of conducting exit interviews is flawed because the information provided by such interviews is gleaned far too late for any practical management response. A better approach, he advises readers, is to ask the same type of questions as those asked in an exit interview "along the way", as a check on organisational culture and to provide opportunities for an appropriate response.

It is important to note that Iggy, in writing Ban the Performance Appraisal, has not intended to provide readers with a set of recipes to manage effectively. His intent is to provoke thought in relation to what might constitute effective management and leadership practice.

And while providing readers with an opportunity to reflect on their own management and leadership practices, which is most likely the key reason for purchasing this book, there is a secondary reason, which is philanthropic in nature. The proceeds of this book will be used to support two significant charities for which the author has a strong passion for: Rotary International and Beyond Blue.

I congratulate Iggy on his generosity in both sharing his own management experience and on his support of two important charities.

Emeritus Professor Gary Martin
CEO and Executive Director of Australian Institute of Management (WA)

Previously:
Senior Deputy Vice Chancellor Murdoch University in Western Australia
Chairperson of Perth Education City, Western Australia
Emeritus Professor of Murdoch University Business School and Zhejiang University of Technology (Zhejiang Province, China)
Honorary Professor at Guangdong University of Business Studies (Guangdong Province, China)

Acknowledgements

This book would not have come to fruition without the generous assistance of others along the way.

Firstly, I would like to thank my wife, my soul mate, Judy who has provided "wise owl" advice and always kept my feet on the ground. My children, Emma, Jayden, Georgia and Nathan who put up with my antics and endure the dreaded annual family Christmas newsletter.

My particular thanks to Sandy Smith for encouraging me to get off my backside and start writing this book rather than just talking about it.

The Rotary Club of Matilda Bay, Western Australia for inspiring me to commence the speaking and presentation circuit on the topic. Also for the club's support of the project and help in getting Rotary International as a distribution partner.

Of course, all proceeds from this book support Rotary International and Beyond Blue. Thanks also to Beyond Blue for its support.

My particular thanks to my good friend, Phil Swain for getting my speaking program underway with the introduction of two national environmental health conferences.

The project simply would not have worked without the generosity and spirit shown by previous employees and managers who shared their personal stories and feedback in the book. To personal friends and colleagues I have quoted in the book, I thank you for your contribution and wisdom.

I would like to thank and acknowledge all my previous managers and all the people who have ever worked in my organisations. You have in some way taught me about the possibility of a great workplace culture.

I would also like to thank Dr Sally-Ann Jones who has been a valuable collaborator on this project and inspired me to push on and get this book written. My sincere appreciation to Jane Carew-Reid for her final review and edit of the book. Also, thank you to Rachel Cassotti who donated her valuable time for the graphic design and organising the printing of the book. You guys are inspirational.

Finally my sincere gratitude and appreciation to Emeritus Professor Gary Martin for taking the time out of his very busy schedule to pen the foreword of this book. Truly amazing.

I hope this book inspires you to develop your own insight and wisdom.

Iggy Tan

Introduction

Introduction

It was 4.05am and I woke with a jolt. I was in Buenos Aires, Argentina on a business trip. I don't know what woke me from a deep sleep but I had an uneasy feeling. I tossed and turned and couldn't get back to sleep. Eventually I got up and started to check my emails on my phone. There it was, an email sent only 15 minutes earlier, advising me of the devastating news. By about 10am, I was on a plane to China.

The email wrote of a bad accident in my newly-built plant in China that took place while I slept. A completely unpredicted pipe rupture after an extended power failure that caused eleven employees to be badly burnt from exposure to hot brine liquid. Emergency procedures were undertaken on the site and the injured were rushed to nearby hospitals with life-threatening burns and other injuries. I had immediately boarded a plane and 24 hours later, I was on site in China.

At the same time, my general manager of technology also boarded a plane from Australia and we met to provide assistance to the site management team. We visited our injured colleagues in hospital. Many were badly burned, with some suffering burns to more than 80% of their body. We also talked to and supported their families as best we could.

For me, it was a moving experience and probably the lowest point of my career as a leader. In China there are often limited nursing staff in the hospitals, so our site staff organised themselves onto shifts to help the nurses clean wounds, change bandages and comfort their colleagues. Each injured employee had two work colleagues at their bedside. Other staff organised themselves on rosters to look after the families of their injured colleagues. All the staff pulled together as one family unit. We provided the best care possible and transferred the injured to the top hospitals in Shanghai.

Sadly, two of our colleagues passed away due to major infection resulting from the burns. As you can imagine, this was devastating for the families and caused a shockwave of grief and sadness that ran through the entire organisation. It was heart-wrenching for me. I felt responsible and blamed myself for the injured staff and for the two people who died while under my charge.

Following the incident, we engaged an international incident and grief counselling group to help all on-site employees deal with their emotions. They counselled many employees and after the sessions provided me with feedback. The feedback stuck in my head for a long time and backed up my passion about the importance of culture.

The counsellors said that they'd seen many organisations around the world during incident counselling, but they'd never experienced such a unique culture in an organisation such as ours. The strength, closeness and family-type culture was unique and would be the strength that would see the organisation recover. The organisation did recover but the workmates who were lost have not been forgotten.

That feedback still rings in my head today.

What makes you happy at work?

First, let me tell you I'm not a management consultant and I'm not trying to sell you a management system or framework. I'm a chemical and mining CEO with 30 years of experience in managing projects and companies in Australia. I have a passion for creating high-performing workplace cultures.

If you're looking for a prescriptive answer or the top 10 rules to make your workplace zing, this is not the book for you. Instead, I've written it to encourage you to think about what will work for you and what makes you (and your staff, if you're a manager) happy and productive in the workplace. Hopefully it'll give you the confidence to implement change at whatever level you are in your company.

The title of the book, "Ban the Performance Appraisal", is purposely controversial but it is only one minor aspect of what can be changed to support a more open, inclusive, happy, kind and compassionate workplace environment.

In life there are no right or wrong answers. Things have to be tested – and some will and some won't work. This is just part of managing the journey of human behaviour.

My background…
During my career, I've worked in large multinational companies as well as medium and small ones. In the first 11 years of my career I worked with a big American multinational based in Western Australia but I spent time in the UK and the USA as well. I quickly progressed into management since graduating from university – in fact within a year or two.

In case you're interested, I hold a Master of Business Administration from the University of Southern Cross, a Bachelor of Science from the University of Western Australia and I'm a graduate of the Australian Institute of Company Directors.

I consider myself lucky to have been born with a natural talent in managing, communicating and working with people. It's a useful talent to have at work, but doesn't necessarily transfer to the home, where I have a wife and four children, three of whom are young adults also experiencing the highs and lows of work. In fact my wife Judy often tells me that I may be the CEO at work but she is the CEO at home. In other words, "toeing the line" at home is also another natural talent of mine.

I left the chemical industry at plant manager level and moved into the mining industry. For the next nine years I worked at the general manager level in relatively large Australian mining companies. Throughout this time, I experienced how the operations of these large companies ran, noting the various management practices and human resource management – I thought there had to be a better way. It was very frustrating as a manager and there was a high degree of scepticism from the workforce.

I questioned the management theory and research from my personal experiences and decided that we needed to get back to basic management.
We have overcomplicated management practices and we've consequently created political, bureaucratic, unhappy workplaces. The theme of "less is more" will be a unifying thread throughout this book.

After working at the general manager level, I moved to CEO level and for the next decade I was able to implement some of my ideas into the organisations that I led. Over my 30 years' management experience and study of management, I've come to believe we can develop some alternative views and techniques for managing people better, in turn producing happy, dynamic and highly effective organisations with a social conscience.

High-performing, kind, compassionate and happy organisations...

In this book I share my ideas on the importance of workplace culture in driving high-performing organisations. In Chapter 1 (Workplace culture is behaviour), I discuss the current disconnection in some organisations between published values and the actual behaviours of the organisation. The culture of any group is the actual behaviour and actions of the group solely driven by the leader or the CEO. The notion that published values help create workplace culture is flawed. By not having published values, it makes managers and leaders focus more on what message their actual behaviour is sending to their workforce.

In Chapters 2 and 3 (Ban the performance appraisal; Reward team outcomes), I discuss the idea that through the use of performance appraisals and reward systems for individual performance, we have accidentally created competitive and "blame" workplace cultures. These cultures are not conducive to building effective team work in organisations. We need to revise our reward structures from self-centred, individual performance-based, to team performance and outcomes-based, where individuals are encouraged to help each other to achieve the team objectives.

In Chapter 4 (Open, honest, transparent communication), I suggest that this type of two-way communication is imperative for any aspiring high-performing organisation. Unfortunately, manipulation and control of information is a sport today for managers and tends to build political and bureaucratic workplaces. I suggest a flat, direct structure for communication, which breaks down these information gatekeepers.

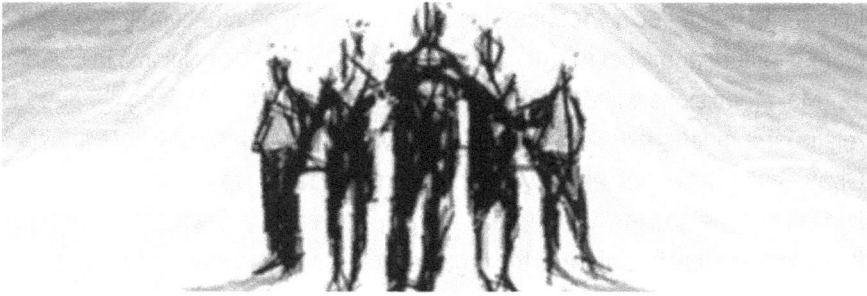

Our management precept is based on the idea that people are motivated by objectives and financial rewards. In Chapter 5 (What really motivates people?), I challenge our reliance on objectives and financial rewards as motivators. In my experience I have come to understand that "warm fuzzies" motivate people, actually, people motivate people. We need to foster managers and leaders that inspire and motivate our people.

In Chapter 6 (Job descriptions are blueprints for silos), I encourage managers to discard the job description, as they encourage silo thinking and behaviour in employees. People become too focused on their individual compartments, whereas they should be doing "whatever it takes" to help others achieve the team targets.

In Chapter 7 (Ban the exit interview), I encourage organisations to ban exit interviews as they are a waste of time. Those important questions should be asked of employees before they leave the organisation. Instead, regular use of team effectiveness surveys (Chapter 8, Take a health check) is a good way to judge the health of the workplace culture.

In Chapter 9 (Mission to Mars and back), I discuss the value of the dreaded mission statement used by many companies. Unfortunately, they serve no purpose and they all look like they came out of a mission statement generator. On the other hand, simple vision statements with powerful imagery are ideal to harness the energy of the workforce and inspire the organisation's overall objectives.

In order to make decisions without fear, an organisation must firstly have a "no blame" culture and a belief that there are no right or wrong decisions. In Chapter 10 (Make decisions without fear), I explain how in decision-making we need to rely on the most important skill that we have failed to nurture: innate intuition. Chapter 11 (Throw out the CV when recruiting) encourages organisations to not find the best person for the role when recruiting, which is a flawed concept, but to find someone that best fits into the organisation. Someone that will help grow the workplace culture. Once again innate intuition is encouraged.

Chapter 12 (Having to dismiss employees) discusses the way we treat our people when we make them redundant. There is often little respect and dignity shown in this process, despite the prominent values in our value statement. Finally, in Chapter 13 (Two steps ahead) I consider how success stems from positive thinking and being "two steps ahead", which creates very proactive workplace cultures.

Employees are fatigued by the plethora of management initiatives that have surfaced over the decades, Chapter 14 (Time to get back to basics). I encourage organisations to strip back the complicated systems that have taken our managers and supervisors away from basic people management. Let's stop wasting our precious time and resources measuring and evaluating and instead allow and trust our managers to do their job.

Real and proven...

Everything I advocate or discuss in this book I have implemented in the organisations I've managed over the last 10 years of my career. The largest was a mining/chemical company with 350 employees and contractors spread across five countries around the world. As CEO of this and other organisations, I have had the opportunity to put these theories and philosophies into practice and demonstrate the creation of happy, dynamic and highly-effective organisations; they are proven and they work.

It's not perfect but it works

Early influences...

In the early part of my management career, and as I was completing my Master of Business Administration, I read and researched several management books, ideas and philosophies. The one person who had the most influence and resonated with my views on team work was Ricardo Semler. He is best known for his radical form of industrial democracy and corporate re-engineering. His 1993 book Maverick addresses the transformation of Semco, a Brazilian company of which he was CEO and majority partner. This book had the most influence on my team based approach to management.

Under Semler's ownership, Semco's revenue grew from US$4 million in 1982 to US$212 million by 2003. Semler's innovative business management policies have attracted widespread interest around the world. He was listed among Time Magazine's 1994 global 100 young leaders; and was named Brazilian businessman of the year in 1990 and in 1992. Semler advocates a decentralised, participatory style of management and leadership.

What I like about Semler is that he was able to put his ideas and philosophies into practice while he was the CEO and owner of the businesses he managed. The opportunity to put his theories into practice by testing them in real life added credibility to Semler's work.

Test for yourself...

I'm not trying to convince you of anything, I just hope some of my ideas spark some good ones of your own in your approach to management, or even in your own place of employment. I hope they'll prompt you to assess everything you do at work to see if there is a net benefit for the workplace.

For instance, just because everyone else might use performance appraisals, doesn't mean they're necessarily useful. Instead of just accepting the management theories, test them for yourself. If they work for your team then go ahead, if they don't work then try something else.

Not too prescriptive...

I don't intend to be too prescriptive. I suggest that people agree on a workplace philosophy and try to nut out something that is right for them. I also don't intend to provide many evidence-based references to support my ideas. They're basically my personal views from my own experience and you don't have to agree with them. In fact, you should disagree along the way. That is part of developing your personal wisdom and insight on the subject.

I would be disappointed if you did not disagree with me

In case, while reading, you feel that my tone may be anti-HR (human resources), I assure you that I am not. I have very dear friends who are dedicated HR professionals and do a great job. HR is only the reflection of the management of an organisation and its philosophy and views. Just like safety, accounting, finance or marketing, HR is a service function that is vital to the management of an organisation. The responsibility of managing employees is always and will always be with supervisors and managers not with HR. The lines have often been blurred in some organisations.

Supporting people around the world...
What prompted me to write and publish this book is that all proceeds will support two important charity organisations that I am passionate about: Rotary International and Beyond Blue.

Rotary International is an international service organisation of which I'm a member. Leadership and expertise from all different disciplines are applied to social issues to promote change. We do great work all around the world, the most successful being the eradication of polio.

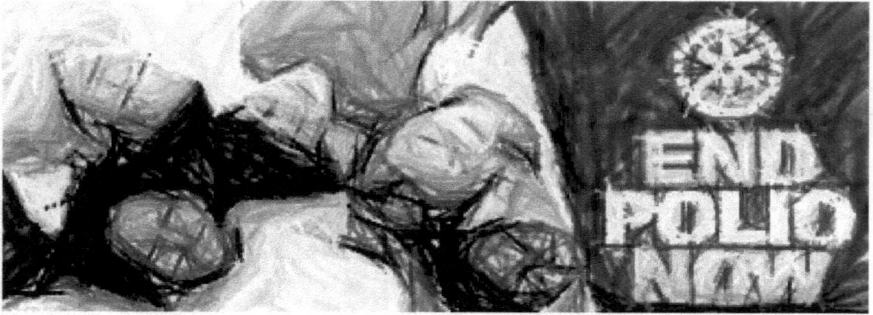

Beyond Blue is a non-profit Australian organisation working to address issues associated with depression, anxiety disorders and related mental disorders, conditions which are becoming more prevalent today. In fact, one million Australians suffer from depression and nearly two million suffer from anxiety. We lose about seven Australians every day to suicide. Almost half the people reading this book would suffer from a mental illness in their lifetime.

So thank you for buying this book, as the proceeds support both of these important charity organisations.

—————————◗◉◖—————————

Chapter 1
Workplace culture is behaviour

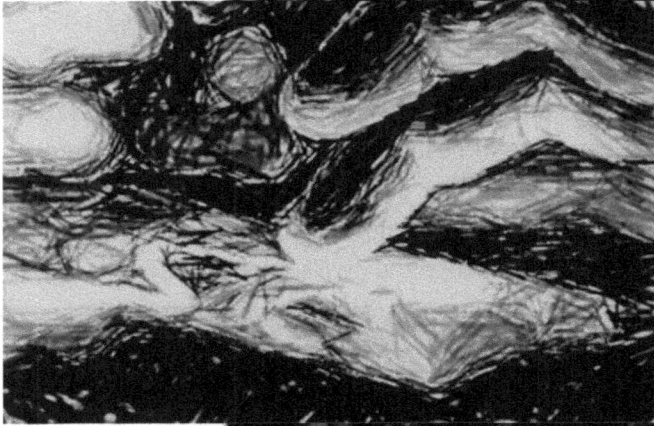

Workplace culture is behaviour

Workplace culture establishes the norms of an organisation's behaviour and shared values. Many organisations treat the creation and maintenance of their workplace culture in a cavalier manner. Either they pay lip service to the kind of culture they aspire to, but don't do much about it, or worse, ignore workplace culture completely.

Often the culture of the workplace is very difficult to define or describe. It's invisible; unique to one's workplace and very difficult to convey to others. Asking an employee to describe his or her workplace culture is like asking a fish to describe water. The fish isn't even aware of its environment because it is swimming in it and is completely oblivious to its presence. Others say that culture is more like a cloud: you know it's there, but it's nearly impossible to grasp.

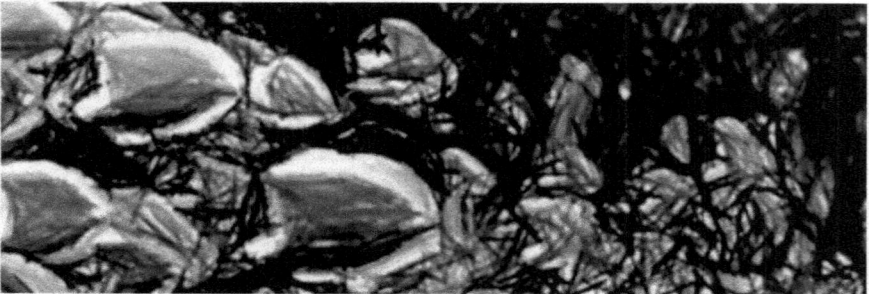

Some describe workplace culture as underlying values, beliefs and principles. Others describe culture as practices and behaviour that reinforce those basic principles. The best description I have heard in describing workplace culture is **"the way we do things around here"**. My belief is that culture is the actual behaviour and actions of individuals or groups in an organisation. The actual way we communicate, the way we reward our people, the way we reprimand, the way we terminate employees, the way we celebrate successes, the way we compete, the way we help each other. The most important of these behaviours is the direct and **actual behaviour of the CEO or leader** of the organisation.

Role of CEO or leader...

The CEO's key responsibility is to set and carry out the strategic plans of that organisation, as advocated/endorsed by the board. In profit organisations, one of the CEO's main concerns is to increase value for the organisation's members. Leading an organisation is a big job; it is a lot harder than it looks! In fact, like all leadership done well, it looks like nothing. We generally fail to understand the profound impact a CEO has on the culture and value system of a company.

"The CEO is the face of the organisation. That means that everything they do, whether at work, at the store or elsewhere – both good and bad – will reflect on the organisation"
Danni Robbins (CEO)

Disconnect with published values...

We are often tempted to articulate the underlying values and beliefs that we desire within our organisation. We create 'value' or 'belief' statements, which are often displayed prominently around the office. I can admit I have done this myself many times! Like the mission statement, these corporate value declarations essentially all look and sound the same.

It doesn't really matter what anyone writes in these "wishful thinking" value statements. The true values of the company's culture come from "the actual way we do things around here"; and usually this stems from the way the CEO behaves. Problems often occur when the actual (not wished) behaviours of the CEO and his executive team don't match the published values. This creates a disconnection and distrust within the organisation, which pervades throughout the workplace.

Any leader and manager – and employee as well – wants to know how to create the kind of harmonious and productive culture they desire. The answer is easy: you, as a manager, leader or employee need to behave it. Yes, it is that simple: your behaviour determines the culture; lead by example.

Peter Levine, a lecturer at MIT, says that despite the best intentions, companies often become culturally dysfunctional. This occurs when leadership has a perception about the culture that conflicts with reality, or leadership behaves differently than what might be written down, according to Peter.

"The organisation reflects the behaviour and characteristics of the CEO, and that establishes the culture. Foster an environment of open communication and the organisation inherits a culture of open communication. Operationally detailed? The organisation becomes operationally detailed. Political? The organisation becomes political. Curse a lot? The organisation curses. Angry? The organisation gets angry. Have a big office? Everyone wants a big office. It doesn't matter what's written on a coffee mug or on a 'culture' slide, what you do as a CEO, day in and day out, and how you behave will define your company's culture".

It has been said that the real 'turning point' for American multinational corporation General Electric's transformation in the 1990's came when CEO and chairman Jack Welch publicly announced to his senior managers that he had fired two business leaders for not demonstrating the new behaviours of the company, despite having achieved exceptional financial results. This sent a very clear message to GE management that culture was not just a soft concept – instead it had tangible outcomes and consequences.

"A strong culture is the backbone of any organisation and the CEO is the standard bearer and the agent of change"

Peter Levine

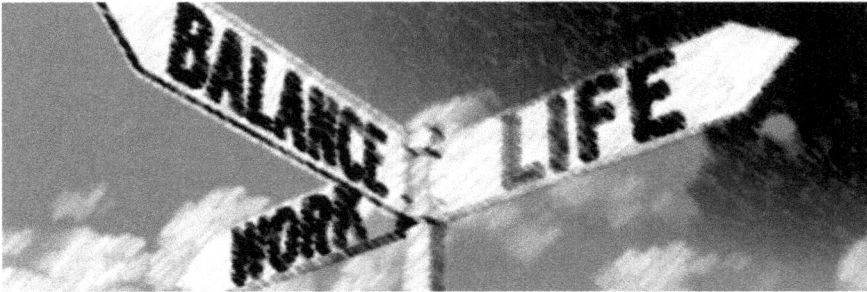

Work-life balance...

Many organisations' values often include good work-life balance approaches to their business. Work-life balance is a concept including proper prioritising between "work" (career and ambition) and "lifestyle" (health, pleasure, leisure, family and spiritual development/meditation). I am sure everyone agrees that the push for a work-life balance naturally results in increased happiness and productivity from employees.

If workplace culture is set by the behaviour of the CEO we need to lead by example in this area. I am sure you will agree that CEO's are probably not the best at representing a good work-life balance. If it is not a behaviour that is demonstrated by the CEO, then it is not likely to eventuate into the workplace culture.

We value good communication...

Good communication is often another value that just about every organisation aspires to have. In Chapter 4, I discuss the importance of open, honest and transparent communication. It is extremely hard work and requires a lot of dedication. The benefits and results are often not obvious. Communication creates the feeling of connectedness or belonging that binds people within a group or organisation. We need that connectedness or belonging in order to become high-performing organisations. If this is a principle that your organisation values then ask yourself "how much time does your leader or CEO spend on communication?"

Respect and dignity?

You'd probably agree with me that one of the most commonly-listed value in a company value statement is "we treat our employees with respect and dignity" – a great value to aspire to and vital for good workplace culture. The problem is that it often doesn't reflect what really happens. Just cast your mind back to the last time your organisation made someone redundant. Did the company treat that person with respect and dignity or did they march them out the door?

I don't know about you but I can't understand how in one instance an employee is regarded as valuable and trusted and then worthless and distrusted the minute they are made redundant. What about the years of service and loyalty that employee has given to the company?

Sacked by SMS...

Recently in Australia there have been instances of workers being made redundant via text message (SMS). In August 2014, 100 workers at a coking coal mine in central Queensland were sacked via SMS. A year later, 40 employees in Brisbane were dismissed by a port employer in a midnight email. They woke to discover they didn't have a job to go to. I can't see how this treatment is an example of treating employees with respect and dignity. One of the coal company's values was listed online for all to see: "We act in an honest and ethical manner".

Among the port company's listed core values and beliefs, under the sub-heading of Communication and Consultation read: "High quality, open and truthful communication that is constructive and informative is essential to engaging informed and participative stakeholders including staff, customers, the community, government agencies and importers and exporters." Sending staff a midnight email to tell them they were no longer needed is not exactly "high quality, open and truthful" communication. Employees see this kind of behaviour every day and managers wonder why they distrust value statements.

It might be better to be silent on the desired values and let the behaviours speak for themselves.

Family values...

In the family home there are generally no stated values nailed onto the front door of the house; a family culture is unique to each individual family. Its culture is determined by the members, although it's mostly the parents' behaviours driven by their values.

So if parents believe that reading is important, piles of books are generally floating around the family home. The parents might read to the children from babyhood and talk about books with their youngsters; they spend money, time and effort relating literature and reading to their children. The importance of reading and literature is inherent in that family's culture. But only when you spend some time with that particular family do you notice that aspect of the culture.

Just like a family home, an organisation doesn't need to publish a set of desired values at the front door for all to see. The culture of the family, like that of a workplace is determined over time through behaviour, interaction, discussion and other subtle influences. The culture of the family, good or bad, is strong and affects all its members. In my opinion, workplace culture works the very same way. Printing a list of wishful values and displaying it is not going to do it.

In fact, Financial Times columnist and BBC broadcaster Lucy Kellaway found in 2015 that 17 of Britain's top 100 companies "get along fine without listing corporate values".

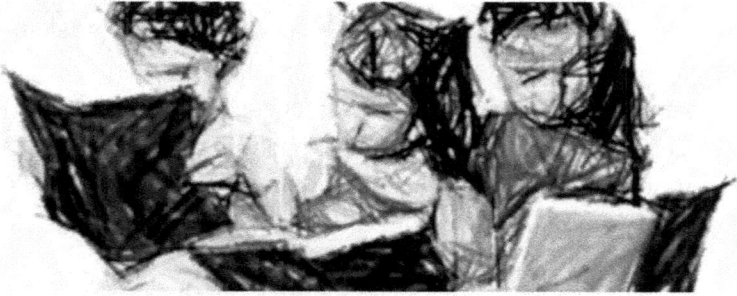

What you sow is what you reap...

At the outset, I must say that there are no good or bad workplace cultures, just consequences. Similarly, there are no good or bad consequences, just consequences. There is a great ancient saying: "what you sow is what you reap". As I discuss the various management ideas in this book, it's important to understand that an appropriate and consistent workplace culture is required primarily. You can't barge ahead with banning performance appraisals and job descriptions and bringing in open, honest communication if your workplace isn't ready.

The relationship between culture and management practices is symbiotic. You need the culture to support the management practices and the management practices create a culture that supports itself. In other words, without the overall philosophy and behaviours combining into culture, none of the management ideas and practices discussed in this book will work in isolation. So just banning the performance appraisal tomorrow after reading this book will not necessarily work.

But you need to create a culture that makes the need for performance appraisals redundant. The next chapter discusses the various aspects of management practice that makes this possible.

Employee comments:
"Upon reflection, after experiencing a number of operations and their management cultures, many think they have a certain culture, however in reality they do not and they do not 'walk the talk'.

This experience for me was the reality of a good, enjoyable and rewarding working environment and one where the workforce was engaged and had a very strong care factor. Not often do you experience that."

Roger Pover (Manager)
Previous employee

It's all about the culture, stupid...

I was speaking about the topic of individual rewards to a group of bankers in London last year. These guys were investment bankers in a high profile bank. They said that in their industry big rewards were given to the deal-makers at the expense of those who don't drive deal outcomes.

These guys seemed to be some of the top performers of their banking organisation. They revealed to me that every year, without fail, the bank's target was to get rid of the bottom 10% of the workforce. This "dog-eat-dog" incentive structure was a good thing for these bankers as it drove them to perform.

I asked them what it was like to work there, to which they all agreed, *"It's an absolutely horrible place to work".*

We essentially promote blame cultures...

Organisations are not only preoccupied but obsessed with establishing clarity, measurement and accountability within the workforce. Fundamentally, if you think about it, this represents a "blame" culture. Who does the organisation blame when something goes wrong or when we fail?

Yves Morieux (Boston Consulting Group) in a Ted Talk presentation ("How too many rules at work keep you from getting things done") (Jul 2015) says that an overload of rules, processes and metrics keeps us from doing our best work together.

"All the human intelligence put into organisation design about structures, processes, systems, 40-80% of their time is wasted. We are working harder and harder, longer and longer on less and less value adding activities.

"This is what is killing productivity and what makes people suffer at work. Our organisations are wasting human intelligence. They have turned against human effort."

Mentally healthy workplaces...

At the beginning of this book I discuss creating compassionate, kind and happy workplaces. Throughout the book I discuss how the management systems that we have implemented have arguably created competitive and "blame" work cultures. These cultures may not be conducive for building a mentally healthy, team-based workplace.

I don't know if it has contributed to the mental health of our employees in the workplace, but today we are seeing more and more absenteeism, presenteeism (working longer hours) and compensation claims due to mental health conditions. Untreated depression results in over six million working days lost each year in Australia.

According to a PWC report on mental health in the workplace (funded by Beyond Blue), the impact of mental health conditions is measured as the total cost of absenteeism, presenteeism and compensation claims estimated in one year across all industries. In Australia, this is estimated to be approximately $10.9 billion per year. This comprises $4.7 billion in absenteeism, $6.1 billion in presenteeism and $145.9 million in compensation claims.

3-4 days off work per month for each person experiencing depression

Over 6 million working days lost each year in Australia

12 million days of reduced productivity each year

The report also states that every dollar spent on effective workplace mental health actions may generate $2.30 in benefits to an organisation. These benefits are derived from a reduction in presenteeism, absenteeism, and compensation claims.

According to the PWC report, the number one critical success factor for creating a mentally healthy workplace is "commitment from senior organisational leaders and business owners – a visible, long-term commitment to mental health in the workplace".

Culture can change very quickly...

As mentioned previously, the true values of the culture come from behaviours of the leadership team. What happens when there is a change in CEO or leader; how long does the prevailing workplace culture last before it changes? What I learnt is whilst there is a lot of effort to develop and sustain the kind of workplace you desire as a leader, the minute you stop or leave the organisation, that culture doesn't necessarily persist. Culture is not permanent, in fact it can change very quickly with a new leader.

Employee comments:
*"When I worked in the previous company where the culture was set by the CEO, the company ran smoothly and "automatically".
I noticed a dramatic change of company culture only a few months after the CEO resigned."*

Dr Jingyuan Liu (Manager)
Previous employee

Yes, I fall into the same trap...

As I mentioned before, it doesn't really matter what we say in the "wishful thinking" value statements. Whilst we understand that behaviour sets the agenda for workplace culture, when you have larger organisations, how do you convey and effect the culture more widely without writing values down on paper? This is a constant dilemma of mine and I don't know the answer.

I myself have fallen into the same trap of publishing and distributing corporate value statements. Maybe the answer lies in whether we rely solely on these statements to set culture or we accept that it is the "way we do things around here" that sets workplace culture.

In a nutshell...

It doesn't really matter what anyone writes in corporate value statements. The true values of an organisation's culture comes from "the way we do things around here". The most important of these behaviours is the direct behaviour of the CEO or leader/s of the organisation. There is often a huge difference between an organisation's published values and the actual behaviour of the organisation, which causes a disconnection and distrust within the workplace.

It is possible to create an organisation that is happy, compassionate and kind, as well as dynamic and highly-effective – by simply behaving it.

"An organisation's ability to learn, and translate that learning into action rapidly, is the ultimate competitive advantage."

Jack Welch

Chapter 2
Ban the performance appraisal

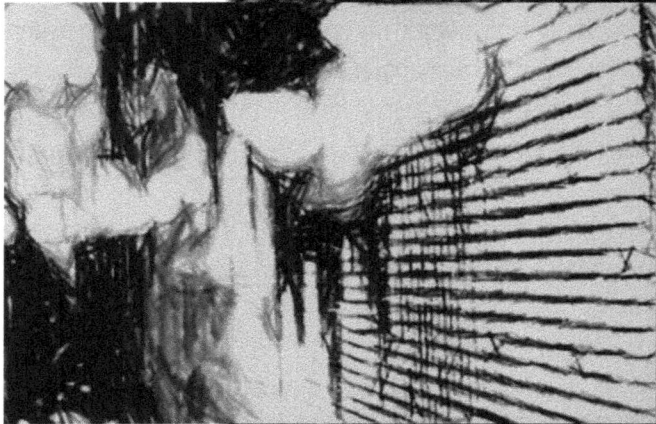

Ban the performance appraisal

A performance appraisal is a formal process that assesses an employee's work performance and productivity. This is usually conducted by company managers on a periodical basis and measured against a set of pre-established criteria and objectives.

I have had to do many in my career. Based on my own experience, I believe there are two camps of people: in the first are those who've found performance appraisals to be worthwhile for their own personal development and motivation. The experience may have compelled them to improve their performance.

In the second camp are those who have found performance appraisals to be unfair, demotivating, frustrating and a waste of time.

Which camp are you in?...

If you sit in the first, then carry on using the performance appraisal and benefit from it. I'm not discouraging anyone from using it if you find it useful. A guy in one of my presentations indicated that he liked the performance appraisal because he often got glowing feedback. *"What's not to like when your boss tells you that you're brilliant?"*, he chuckled.

Unfortunately, when I ask the question during my presentations, about 70-80% of the audience raise their hands to camp two. These people feel that a lot of time is taken up in preparing the appraisals – or taking part in them – with little benefit. In fact, the appraisal can create so much frustration and angst in employees that it becomes counter-productive to improving performance. The process can be destructive and demoralising for employees.

In a Los Angeles Times article, Samuel Culbert, a professor in the Anderson School of Management at the University of California, asked the same question to 62 leadership class MBA students who were full-time professionals. Of the group, 57 of them (92%) described performance appraisals as bad management practice. "It's because they are tired of a system in which bosses manage with a whip; and that whip is the performance review."

Imagine if I was a management consultant and I requested your permission to implement a new management initiative in your workplace. I might add that it was very popular around the world and was supposed to improve the performance of your employees. I'd also have to admit that the benefits of this new initiative weren't guaranteed, and may cause frustration and demotivation to around 70-80% of your workforce. Would you accept? The obvious answer is 'no' so why is this tool used so commonly by many different types of organisations across the globe?

I honestly don't know the answer to that question, except that perhaps we assume it is of benefit because everybody else is doing it.

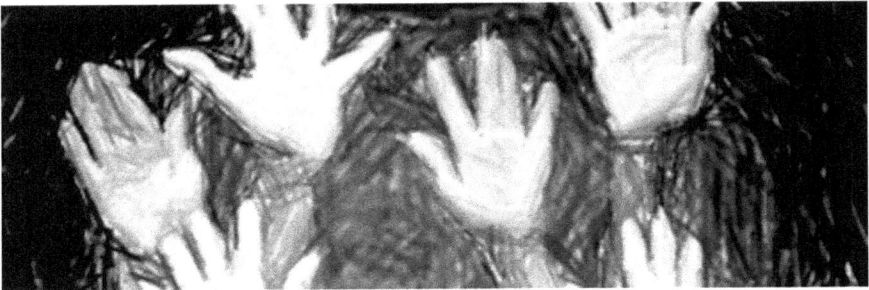

They'd work if they were done properly...
A common response to justify the negative side effects is that performance appraisals, if done properly, can be an effective tool. Despite all the training and instructions we have given our managers, the majority of our workforce still think performance appraisals are a waste of time.

So, rather than blaming the abilities of managers, I suggest that there may be a fundamental flaw in the system. The problem is not with the managers, the problem is with the performance appraisal system itself.

Feedback improves performance...

I don't think anyone would disagree with the notion that feedback helps to improve one's performance. If we agree that feedback is so important why aren't we providing this feedback constantly, regularly and immediately, rather than saving it for once-a-year or every six months?

Why didn't you tell me sooner?

During a performance review how many times have you heard someone, or been that someone thinking "why didn't you tell me about this issue when it happened? I could have done something about it straight away. Instead I find out six months later at my performance appraisal and it's too late for me to do something about it now!"

You can understand why employees get so frustrated. Something that could be fixed, changed or modified at the time has made its way into a formalised appraisal system.

Ladies and gentlemen, when the feedback is delayed it becomes a frustrating and demoralising exercise.

Constant, immediate and dynamic...

Let's go back to one of the simple basics of management – providing constant and immediate (rather than delayed) feedback. So, ban the performance appraisal and create a workplace culture where constant communication is the norm. As a member of staff, you should be able to expect that your boss or supervisor is going to let you know when you do well and when there are areas for improvement, as part of the normal workplace conversation; certainly not collected and stored for a future-dated end of year review.

The coach of a football team doesn't wait until the end of the year to provide feedback to each of the players. The coach gives constant feedback during the game, at the end of the quarter and at the end of the season. The coach is constantly coaching the team and each player knows straight away when they are doing something right or wrong. It's a system that's dynamic and immediate and means the player can do something about it right there and then.

Employee comments:

"We enjoy getting constructive feedback along the way as it enables personal performance to be adjusted on a regular basis. Sometimes negative aspects need to be addressed straight away to enable the person to go forward. I enjoyed not having formal performance appraisals."

Helen Bourke
Previous employee

We need to rate your performance...

People often say to me, "Iggy, the appraisal is designed to measure and rate individual performance. The system needs some measurement from the appraisal process so that we can recommend a reward for that individual employee. Without a rating, how can we compare with the other employees and reward everyone individually?" You'll be aware of the various tools that are used today to measure performance such as scores, alpha ratings, linear scales and description boxes.

Little ratings boxes...

Let's look at a typical rating or ranking system. There are many different types but let's look at one I'm relatively familiar with. It has five boxes ranging from "1" for "excellent", "2" for "good", "3" for "satisfactory" or "meets requirement", "4" for "poor" and "5" for "unsatisfactory".

1	2	3	4	5
Excellent	Good	Satisfactory	Poor	Unsatisfactory

Many organisations tie an annual salary review together with the performance appraisal and the individual rating is used to distribute the available budget increase for the following year. For example, if the target overall average salary increase for the whole business was 2.5% then this is distributed to individuals according to their ratings.

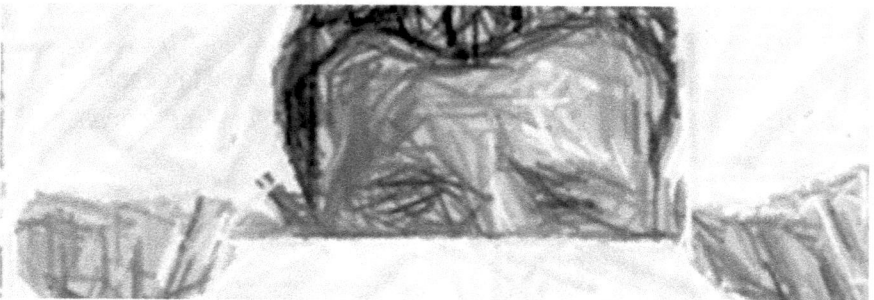

Unfortunately, the use of the rating system comes with many limiting factors. The HR people say that the final ratings in the organisation should reflect a normal distribution (bell) curve.

Bell curve limitations

1	2	3	4	5
Excellent	Good	Satisfactory	Poor	Unsatisfactory

So, if we applied the bell curve distribution for possible ratings, the majority of employees (actually 68% at 1 standard deviation) will be limited to a satisfactory ("3") rating. In other words, while we spend a lot of time and effort preparing and discussing performance, the end result is most likely going to be an "average", "meets requirement" or "satisfactory" ("3") rating for most.

The outer extremities

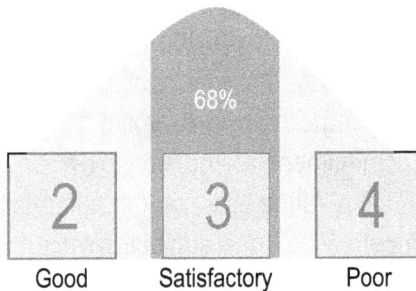

	68%	
2	3	4
Good	Satisfactory	Poor

This is why I believe the actual purpose of the performance appraisal system is to identify the outer extremities of performance: the top versus the poor performers. The system is designed to reward the top performers and reprimand the poor ones. Meanwhile, it frustrates the remaining employees who end up with a "satisfactory" or "meets requirement" rating who think the whole exercise was a waste of time.

This stacks up when I ask people to select a camp and the burning show of hands signals the second camp. If you are in this camp, I am sure your supervisor would have consoled you at some stage, saying that a "meets requirement" score is actually a good outcome. "Try not to think about the score, rather just focus on the feedback and comments", the manager might suggest.

Is this your reaction?

We can't help but focus on the rating...

Whilst we intended for the system to provide valuable feedback to employees and perhaps create a two-way discussion of performance, it has instead become a **negative and demotivating** exercise. Rather than acknowledge the good work and commitment of the employee or areas to work on, employees focus on the final rating as a number one priority! Why? Because we've linked future compensation to this subjective ratings number.

People generally do not like to be rated or given a score for their work or performance. Why, doesn't that help improve their performance in the future? Just as an exercise, after your spouse has prepared dinner and after tasting it tonight, give him or her a score out of ten for their effort. You could raise a score card above your head and see what happens. I suggest you don't do this while sharp knives are in the area!

No matter what the score is, nobody likes to be rated. Ladies and gentlemen, when we created a system that ties rewards to ratings, **feedback became irrelevant**. The feedback blurs into the anxiety of the final rating score.

Global financial services firm Accenture employs 330,000 employees around the world and the company removed the ranking system from their workplace. Accenture's CEO Pierre Nanterme explained, *"All this terminology of rankings – forcing rankings along some distribution curve or whatever – we're done with that, we're going to evaluate you in your role."*

Identify and reward top performers...

As I mentioned previously, the appraisal and reward system is skewed to finding the above average or top performers (rated "1" or "2" in the above example) and rewarding them. It is designed to motivate and reward a small percentage of the workforce but in the process demotivates the rest. In my experience, top performers may not necessarily be good team players. Arguably, they're focused on themselves, their career, and they often create a highly competitive workplace environment.

We have all been taught to believe employees will work harder and more efficiently if we reward them individually. Those that perform well should be remunerated differently from the rest of the group. This encourages everyone to perform at their peak so that they can get the extra 1% pay increase ahead of the others at the end of the year. Our idea of what motivates people is flawed, but more about that later in Chapter 5 (What really motivates people?).

In a Washington Post article, Brian Kropp, HR practice leader for research company CEB reported that, *"Employees that do best in performance management systems tend to be the employees that are the most narcissistic and self-promoting...those aren't necessarily the employees you need, to be the best organisation going forward."*

Rating the children...

Now just to prove a point, I'm going to conduct performance appraisals on my children (you will notice I left my wife out of this, life would not be worth living if I rated her). I have four children, which means my family is nearly as big as some small organisations. My children's ages are 23, 21, 19 and 14. The theoretical performance appraisal goes something like this: *"Mum and Dad have conducted individual performance reviews on everyone's contribution to the family, your attitude, your completion of chores and general contribution to the household".*

I might say, during my eldest daughter Emma's performance appraisal: *"Emma, a great year, you've met all the requirements, completed all your chores and kept your bedroom relatively clean. But you need to improve in your personal laundry efforts. This year we've awarded you a "3" or "satisfactory". We've therefore increased your allowance by an extra $1 per week for your year's effort."*

Emma's rating

 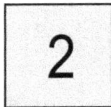   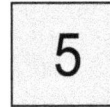

1	2	3	4	5
Excellent	Good	Satisfactory	Poor	Unsatisfactory

And 19 year-old Georgia's performance appraisal? This is what she might hear: *"Georgia, you've done a great job this year. Not only have you done all your chores but you helped mum without being asked. You've been a team player and this has resulted in a great year's effort. We've awarded you a "2" or "good" and we've increased your allowance by an extra $2 per week. Plus, you'll get an extra scoop of ice cream (our bonus system) each dinner time."*

Georgia's rating

    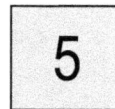

1	2	3	4	5
Excellent	Good	Satisfactory	Poor	Unsatisfactory

What about our eldest son Jayden's performance appraisal? *"Jayden, what an outstanding year. You've met all that is required but you've also demonstrated excellent leadership, especially during the last family camping trip when we got lost. You've helped the rest of the family and so we've rated you a "1" or "outstanding". Your allowance will be increased by an extra $3 per week and you'll get two extra scoops of ice cream every dinner time".*

Jayden's rating

    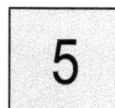

1	2	3	4	5
Excellent	Good	Satisfactory	Poor	Unsatisfactory

And Nathan, the youngest of the family: *"Nathan, we have had issues with your performance this year. Your room is always messy, we have to nag you to do your homework and you're constantly on your Playstation. Unfortunately, we have to rate you a "4" or "poor" and there will be no change to your allowance this year."*

Nathan's rating

  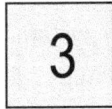  

| Excellent | Good | Satisfactory | Poor | Unsatisfactory |

After the performance appraisal process we reassure the kids to focus on the feedback and comments rather than their rating. And of course this doesn't work as the rating means more money and ice cream and we all know how much we love ice cream. *No children were psychologically harmed in the production of this book.*

When we tied rewards to ratings, feedback became irrelevant...

So what are the children thinking?

"4" is totally unfair

This sucks, it is not worth the extra effort and work

How come Jayden gets two ice creams?

You don't see when Georgia slacks off

Nathan is totally despondent with his rating of "4". He feels that his good work went unnoticed during the year and he's now very worried that he is on the adoption list. Nathan finds the whole process very demotivating.

Emma's annoyed that she got a lower score than Georgia because she believes Georgia is a self-promoter who slacks off. Emma is going to focus on making sure the parents (aka management) notice her true work ethic in the future. Meanwhile Georgia feels her reward is not fair considering she's put in more effort than Jayden. She's annoyed that her efforts are not truly acknowledged or rewarded.

Given the above example, does the system motivate the top performer, in the case of my son Jayden? While he's happy with the rating he received, he's most likely not as happy with his reward. He believes the extra reward (over and above say Georgia's reward) is not worth it compared to the work and effort he has put in. One extra scoop of ice cream and one extra dollar in his allowance does not necessarily motivate him. Jayden will either drop back his effort or look to move to another family.

Another Washington Post article on brain research results suggests that even employees who get positive performance reviews experience negative effects from the process. It often triggers disengagement and constricts their openness to creativity and growth.

Can you imagine what would happen to the dynamics of the family following this so-called performance review? Do you think this exercise would help with the children's individual motivation or encourage them to work as a team?

At home, family disharmony would probably ensue and each child will likely become more competitive and less collaborative. So instigating an appraisal and rewards system in the family seems rather ridiculous. We would create a "blame culture" where, for example, the next time my daughter Georgia fails or needs help, Emma may not help her, instead choosing to highlight her flaws to mum and dad (management). No one will be keen on helping Nathan because he's seen as a liability and will most likely be "managed out" (adopted) of the family.

Dissatisfaction and competition...

The reaction in the family example is exactly how employees are feeling in the workplace. So did we mean to create that much dissatisfaction in the workplace by a seemingly innocent appraisal system? Did we mean to create a competitive workplace? Unfortunately, we've accidentally created a workplace culture where people use blame in order to look good in the next performance review. We've accidentally created a "looking good" culture.

A friend of mine who works in a large organisation said to me that over the years he'd learnt how to look good for the system and therefore get high ratings in performance reviews. He'd learnt how to play the game and consequently he's seen as one of the guys who can get the right attention from the managers. He is now a section manager in this organisation.

Did we mean to create such competitive workplaces?

Performance appraisals are subjective...

We, as managers, often reassure our staff that their performance appraisal is an objective and fair process. Performance appraisal forms have become more and more complex, with many boxes to fill in. A friend of mine who is a manager in a large company said that his review forms were 15 pages long and it took his boss several days to prepare. There were many boxes to tick or cross, and many evaluation criteria to complete, so it must be objective, right?

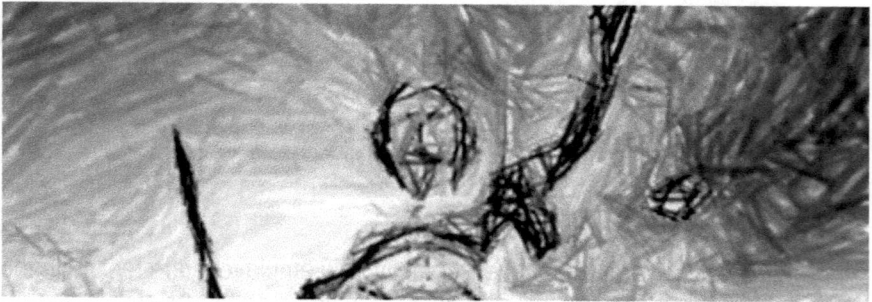

Let's be totally frank here. Performance appraisals are not objective; they never have been and never will be. It doesn't matter how extensive and complicated the forms are, everyone knows the process is totally subjective. The next time you might have to conduct a review, just acknowledge upfront that it is a totally subjective process and that it is just your personal opinion. At least you'll commence the process with some authenticity. It gives the signal that you and your employee may have to agree to disagree.

360 degree feedback...

During one of my presentations someone asked me what I thought of 360 degree feedback tools. Fundamentally, this is a system to reinforce the idea that the appraisal process is an objective process. If a performance appraisal is a waste of time, then a 360° feedback wastes more people's time. *"Instead of one person telling you that you're not a team player, I managed to find three other people to tell you that you're not a team player, in case you don't believe me."*

Performance reviews in the "New Age"...

So where's the future of the performance appraisal heading? I have another friend who is a senior manager at a large multinational organisation with operations in many countries. He told me that the company had taken performance appraisals to the next stage. *"We now enter everything on this online program, which evaluates everyone and produces an overall rating,"* he proudly declared. My reaction to that was *OMG!?* Then, another manager in the same company (also a friend) added, *"Often the program doesn't give you the exact rating you were after but we've worked out how to trick the program to get the rating we think the employee deserves."*

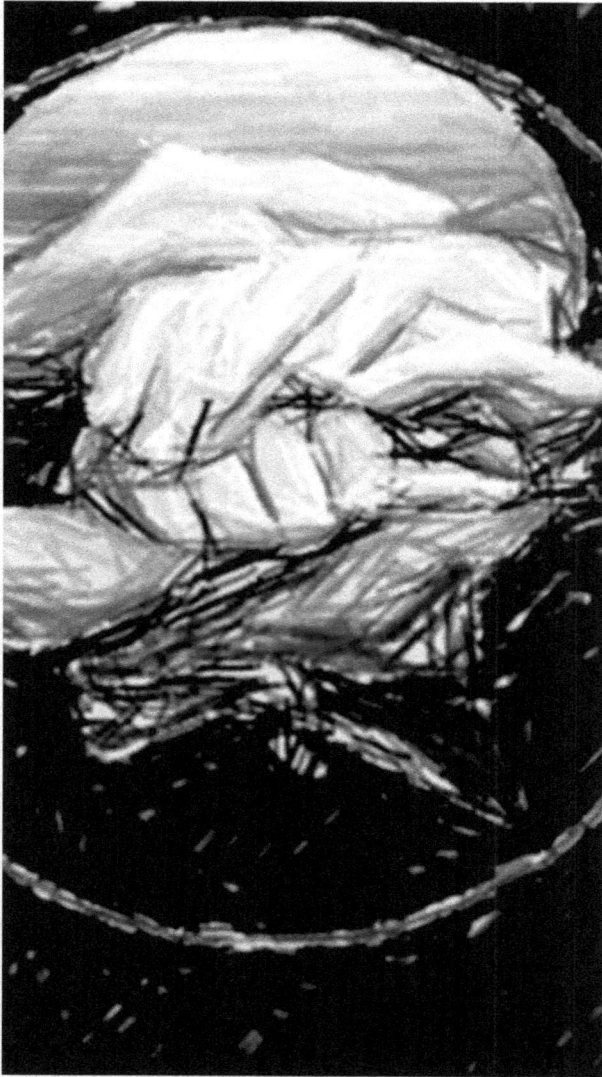

*"Research indicates that employees have three prime needs:
Interesting work; recognition for doing a good job; and being let in on things
that are going on in the company."*

Zig Ziglar

A world without performance appraisals

Just walk into family-run businesses or restaurants, construction or transport companies, courier services, hardware stores, supermarkets, fishing companies, farms, gift shops or day-care centres: thousands and thousands of these privately-run organisations operate throughout the world very efficiently without performance appraisals. They range from small, medium or large family-owned companies that are responsive, dynamic and often very successful.

Just go to one of these family-owned companies and ask them if they conduct performance appraisals for their employees. They're likely to laugh at you because they don't need to. They're less bureaucratic and instead give feedback to their employees that is constant, immediate and if required, on a daily basis.

Management research firm CEB reported in a Washington Post article that the average manager spends more than 200 hours a year on activities related to performance reviews. When you add up those hours, plus the cost of the performance-management technology itself, CEB estimated that a company of about 10,000 employees spends roughly US$35 million (around AU$47 million) a year on conducting performance reviews.

Instead, Professor Samuel Culbert suggests: *"Get rid of the performance review with its boss-dominated, intimidating relationship, and its focus on what hasn't worked in the past".*

Culbert questions: *"Who says you have to do something that damages the relationship between bosses and their subordinates that practically forces employees to be dishonest to their managers, that keeps workers from doing the best they can do, and in the end hurts the bottom line?"*

How do you provide feedback?

If you decided to ditch the performance appraisal, how do you provide feedback to your employees? The same way a classroom teacher provides feedback to students; the same way a coach provides feedback to the players; the same way an owner of a family business provides feedback to their staff; and the same way good leaders manage their people. It is all done **immediately and as required**. It is a very simple process and we certainly do not need another management system to make sure it happens.

> **Employee comments:**
> *"I remember when one of the senior managers was underperforming and after several one-on-one meetings, our CEO brought in the full management team to meet with him, discuss and collaborate on a suitable action plan. This is a great way to build team culture and utilise peer management. There was a tremendous improvement and commitment from this senior manager."*
>
> Anand Sheth (Senior Manager)
> Previous employee

In our organisations we try to provide positive feedback when people do things well, but we need to also be disciplined as managers to provide negative feedback when it is required. As you know, negative feedback is hard to provide and it can sit unpleasantly with people. We must have the courage as managers to address the issues upfront and immediately rather than leave it for the performance appraisal time.

Stop rating people...

The message from my family example is pretty clear in that providing a score to family members causes disharmony and discontentment. So, why then are we happy to perform this same rating system in the workplace? Why would the reactions be any different? The system of rating someone's performance is very subjective; that's why, for example, there are 10 judges in an Olympic Games gymnastic event as the scores are widely varied – or subjective.

Companies today are already starting to question the notion of ranking their employees. According to another Washington Post article, the consulting and accounting giant Deloittes announced that it was piloting a new program in which rankings would disappear. Microsoft stopped its rankings about two years ago, attracting particular attention since it had long evangelised about the merits of its system that judged employees against each other. Adobe, Gap and Medtronic also transformed their performance review process.

We never missed them...

In the four companies that I have led and managed as a CEO in the last ten years, the performance appraisal system was never instigated. Even in the largest company of around 350 people spread across five countries we didn't do one single appraisal in the five years I was at the helm.

We never made a big issue or song and dance about banning it in the organisation. We just never did it, no one missed it nor felt neglected. Instead we saved hundreds of hours each year on activities that would normally be tied up with performance reviews and training sessions, form filling and delivering evaluations to employees.

A "massive revolution"...

The move to abandon the performance appraisal is happening in some of the world's biggest companies. In the US, 6% of Fortune 500 companies, including financial services firm Accenture, have abolished rankings, according to management research firm CEB. Accenture CEO Pierre Nanterme said that the professional services firm has been quietly preparing for this "massive revolution" in its internal operations.

"Imagine, for a company of 330,000 people, changing the performance management process – it's huge," Nanterme said. *"We're going to get rid of probably 90% of what we did in the past."* As mentioned, the firm will remove its once-a-year evaluation process starting in fiscal year 2016. And instead, it will implement a more fluid system in which employees receive timely feedback from their managers on an ongoing basis following assignments. *"The process is too heavy, too costly for the outcome...and the outcome is not great"*, says Nanterme.

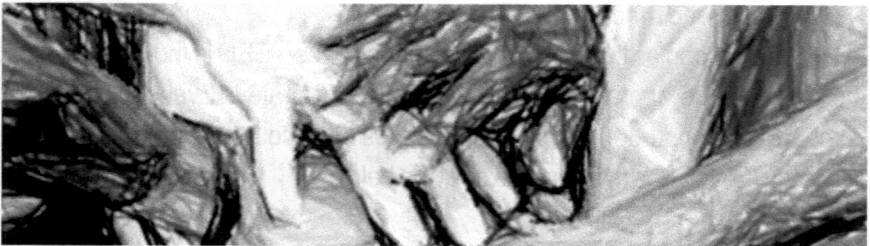

Employee comments:
"Having completed and conducted performance appraisals both with my managers and with my staff, over more than 20 years, I am convinced that for the most part they are a waste of time. In my opinion, approximately 15% of staff find them useful to manage their career progression whilst the majority find them subjective, frustrating, a waste of time and in some cases, demotivating."

Nick Hancock (Sales Manager)
Previous employee

Trust your managers to do their job...

How do we encourage our managers to provide this basic, constant feedback? The answer: create a workplace culture where complex bureaucratic systems with paperwork and procedure, like appraisals, are not in the way of managers and their workforce. Remove these unnecessary systems and most managers will do what they're good at: managing people. After all, we promoted these people to managerial positions due to their skills in people management. Remember, a formal appraisal system takes away the opportunity for constant, immediate, regular feedback.

In a nutshell...

Unfortunately, the majority of employees believe that performance appraisals are a waste of time, demoralising and are of little benefit. In fact, the appraisal can create so much frustration and angst for employees that it becomes counter-productive for improving performance. The performance appraisal system, and our reward system for individual performance, has accidentally created a competitive, looking good and "blame" workplace culture. Ban the performance appraisal and create a workplace culture where informal, regular, timely and immediate feedback is the norm.

Chapter 3
Reward team outcomes

Reward team outcomes

Effective teamwork is one of the most common topics addressed by countless management books and articles. We see on the sporting field that when good teamwork comes into play, the team excels and often wins the game with ease. We also recognise this in our organisations. We are social animals and, like our hunting ancestors, we instinctively understand the notion that "none of us is as good as all of us". In a teamwork environment, people understand and believe that thinking, planning, decisions and actions are better when done co-operatively.

As discussed in the previous chapter, the performance appraisal system and our reward system for individual performance has accidentally created a competitive, "blame" culture, which rarely emphasises true teamwork and collaboration. In order to encourage teamwork, we need to change the reward system to encourage employees to achieve the overall team targets by helping each other. Compensation, bonuses, and rewards must depend on collaborative practices rather than individual contribution and achievement.

Teamwork?

The same scenario as in the family example is exactly what we've established in the workplace. It's interesting that we have created this competitive culture only to then spend time and resources with team-bonding sessions outside the workplace to try and promote teamwork. You know the sessions where group activities, teamwork and trust are encouraged in outdoor exercises; where company staff from all levels come together to play games such as 'tug-of-war' or problem-solve with 'the great race' to encourage team interaction and communication.

How do you truly expect to get real teamwork, as in everyone helping each other to achieve team goals, when we have a culture of competing or "looking good"? Unless we give up the idea of identifying and rewarding individual performance, we can never achieve 'true' teamwork. You get true teamwork when everyone has to pick the stragglers up and get everyone across the line without blame. I suggest the first step in developing teamwork is our internal organisational structures.

Competitive and cut-throat...

How often have you heard organisations claim that they have the top and brightest people in their organisation? What they don't say is that the company is actually not a nice place to work for and everyone is looking after their own career advancements, their bonus, and how to look even better. If this highly competitive, cut-throat environment is where you want to work, that's fine.

However, I think people generally want to work in caring, compassionate and happy workplaces. Yet we've been brought up to believe that the competitive, "survival of the fittest" workplace environment makes us all more efficient. It's not a culture where you could be vulnerable nor is it a culture where people will help to cover for you in the interest of the overall team performance.

How do you expect to get 'true teamwork' when we have a system that rewards individual achievement?

Not everyone wants excitement...

I remember in the early stages of my management career I was based on-site at a chemical processing plant. The plant's final product was loaded via three bagging stations by an operator per station. The job for the operators of each train was to put a bag onto a spout then press the button for 'load'. The bag would then fill with product before being lifted onto a conveyor belt. The operator would repeat this same task for 12 hours a shift. It was an important part of the process: if no product was bagged, no product would go to customers and there'd be no revenue for the company.

As a manager I thought there'd be opportunities for job rotation so that these guys would be able to learn other skills and wouldn't be so bored at work. After trying to implement job rotation on the whole plant I encountered strong resistance. These packers eventually came to me and said that they'd been doing the packing job for many years; they enjoyed it and didn't want to swap or learn any other jobs. They didn't want to change. The best part of being a packer, they told me, was that they didn't have to think too much.

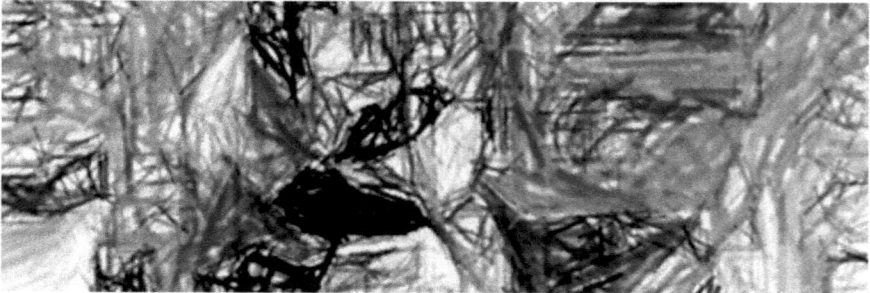

At first I couldn't understand why anyone would want to do such a boring job. I later realised that people are different and those guys were as important to the team's success as the people who were more ambitious, more skilled and more interested in learning. So, early on in my management career I learnt to embrace the differences in people. I learnt that what I may find boring in a job was actually okay for these packers. This was my first lesson in teamwork.

Can people change?

This is a fundamental question that is the essence of management philosophy. Do we try to change people to what we want? When asked this question, a friend's wife replied, "*People change but you can't change them*". These are very wise words indeed.

I'm sure you reading this have had many years of pure frustration when trying to change people either around you or people that work for you. The frustration makes you unhappy and affects your performance as a manager, leader and colleague. You fundamentally can't force people to change so give up that idea and let that notion go.

We start in our relationships thinking that we can change our spouses. After many years of trying and much grief (just ask my wife), you realise that people don't necessarily change. It's probably easier to accept them as they are, if you can work with them to a certain extent and see something positive in them.

Embrace everyone...

An approach that works in companies I've managed is to embrace everyone in the team and accept that not all can be above-average performers. Accept that some will be quiet achievers, some will be clock-watchers, some will do an okay job, and some will do a great job. Accept that some will use initiative and some won't have initiative. Some are great communicators and some are not. Accept that some will have ambition and want to expand their skills while some are happy to just do their job – like the packers. The fabric of all types of people that make up a team reflect society and the sooner we can all embrace the concept that we can't all be high-flyers the better.

No one's perfect but the team can be

Out with the bad apples...

So, with this embracing philosophy, does that mean that we should put up with employees who can't do their job or who are disrupters of team harmony and performance? The simple answer is 'no'. If a worker impacts negatively on team output, performance or morale, then you manage them out as you might have done in the past. There's no change there. The performance management process is exactly the same. But instead of waiting for the annual performance appraisal, you provide and record a feedback and performance plan straight away. It becomes more immediate and decisive instead of the drawn-out process of annual reviews just to build up a case.

Teams work...

There is a great saying about teams: there are no "I's" in TEAM but there is always an "A" hole. Your job as a manager is to weed them out. A team is built up of very different types of people with varying skills, education, ambition and commitment. If, as a manager, you stop trying to change everyone to being top performers (like yourself) the frustration of management will disappear and you can actually focus on getting the whole team engaged and motivated and in the process, performing and achieving.

*"Everyone talks about building a relationship with your customer.
I think you build one with your employees first."*

Angela Ahrendts

Team-based targets...

It is possible to reward team performance and reinforce team behaviour. Set some global targets and if they are achieved then everyone in the entire team gets rewarded equally. So, if it's a 2% salary increase for the next year, then the CEO down to the cleaner gets the same quantum. This philosophy drives every team within the organisation to work together to achieve the overall targets.

There will be temptation to try and differentiate the importance and impact of teams within the organisation but remember it takes all teams to make the overall organisation perform. The system is very simple: give everybody the same reward, from the CEO to the gate person. The message is also very consistent: *"We are all valued equally and everyone plays a part in making the whole organisation work effectively"*. Of course the CEO has more complex tasks but this is reflected in his or her higher pay scale.

"If you have a workforce that enjoys each other, they trust each other, they trust management, they're proud of where they work - then they're going to deliver a good product"

Jeff Smisek

Change the environment...

The behaviour and culture of the workplace creates the change that is required in people. Please don't get me wrong, my organisations aren't perfect places like nirvana. Please don't think that I don't struggle with managing people and their behaviours or idiosyncrasies. It's an ongoing battle and people management remains a constant challenge for me and probably for every manager or supervisor.

**You can create the environment or workplace culture
that creates change in people**

Complete teamwork...

So let's imagine an organisation that sets group targets and rewards everyone equally when those targets are achieved. This system drives "complete" teamwork by encouraging people to stop creating competition, stop working in silos and instead develop a "whatever it takes" attitude.

If only one department within an organisation achieves all their goals it means nothing if the entire company falls over; or, if the goals are achieved at the expense of other departments, it doesn't make sense. Rewarding for individual performance may drive self-centred and selfish, competitive behaviour. In setting group goals, do so in such a way that many teams and groups within the company are linked and have to work together to achieve success. Set high standards and trust your employees and colleagues and they'll live up to your high expectations.

"We're all working together; that's the secret"

Sam Walton

Employee comments:

"I felt the management team were very much managing in a culture of real teamwork. We were trusted to do our work without getting involved in producing low value KPIs or being tied down with performance reviews etc.

As a manager, I felt that we had the trust from executive management and they understood that we knew what we needed to do to manage the operation. They were there to support us and not to micro-manage us.

We were given the autonomy to manage, which allowed us to foster that management culture/philosophy and transfer it across the operation. In my view employees at the mine site were generally happy with their employment conditions and particularly the work environment."

Dr Jingyuan Liu (Manager)
Previous employee

In a nutshell...

In order to achieve effective teamwork, we need to change the reward system and encourage employees to help each other to achieve the overall team targets. Compensation, bonuses, and rewards must depend on collaborative practices rather than individual contribution and achievement.

Teamwork is about embracing the differences in people. The fabric of all types of people that make up a team reflect society and the sooner we can embrace the concept that we can't all be high-flyers the better. Set global targets and if they are achieved then everyone in the entire team gets rewarded equally. People generally want to work in these caring, compassionate and happy workplaces.

Chapter 4
Open, honest, transparent communication

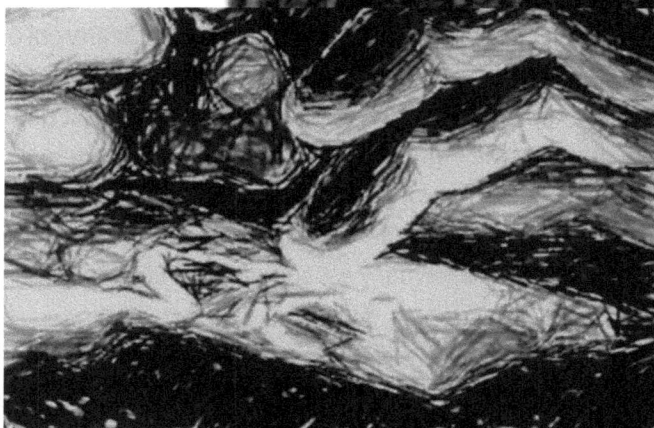

Open, honest, transparent communication

The next topic I would like to cover is communication within the workplace and how to improve it. Every management book will stress the importance of communication or information flow relating to effective organisations. But do we really understand why communication is so essential?

Yes, we need immediate information to be able to carry out our jobs as effectively as possible. For example, if I was an accounts payable employee, I would need to have all the information relating to my department and specific information about the payable process and my internal and external customers. But why might it be important for me to be aware of the bigger picture, other departments, the organisation's overall objectives, aspirations, achievements, its external environment, and the many aspects of what makes the organisation tick?

Some people believe that this level of information engagement is "nice to have" but not necessarily essential for employees to be effective at their job. In my experience, communication is the most critical aspect of building happy, effective and efficient organisations. It's the first thing I target when I take over an operation or a company.

'You don't need to know'...
In these operations, I usually find that communication is extremely poor and there is poor engagement with employees. These organisations are often secretive and political and information is often manipulated and controlled by managers. These communication and information manipulators or gate-keepers are the resistance to building open, honest and transparent organisations.

These workplaces are often described as having an "on a need to know basis" communication culture. I'm sure you've heard the mantra before: *"it is a need to know basis and you don't need to know"*. In my experience, there's a tendency for some managers to not want their subordinates to know as much or more than themselves. Perish the thought, what would their value be as managers!? Generally, the biggest driver is the "looking good" principle. We are all competing to "look good" to the leaders of our organisation.

Face to face...

When you're brought in as a leader to bring about change and improvement in plants and companies, which I have done, you need to have the whole workforce on board, engaged and motivated. You can only do that with constant, open, honest, two-way and face-to-face communication, bypassing the organisation's established, manipulated political systems. I'm sure you've experienced organisations that are political and bureaucratic and you know what it's like to work in them. It zaps your vitality resulting in declining job satisfaction and unhappiness at work.

Chinese whispers...

I believe we need a new communication structure that breaks the filtering and funnelling of information. In order to promote performance or change, the workforce needs to share the leader's vision, passion and energy. But how can this happen when we're playing a game of corporate Chinese whispers?

Most of us have played this game as children. For those who haven't, let me describe how it is played. The idea is to pass on a sentence like "The deer in Canada love playing in the snow just before the sun rises each day". This is passed on by whispering into the ear of the person next to you. That person then whispers to the next person and so on. By the time the final person gets the information they have to say the sentence out loud for everyone to hear. There are usually bouts of laughter as the final message being spoken aloud is something like: "My son loves playing guitar and eating rice in Canada". We think this is a silly and funny game but we are playing this game in our organisations today.

See the whites of your eyes...

In Leadership 101, we learn that people need to see the passion in a leader's eyes, the enthusiasm in their voice and to feel the energy of their conviction as their head of organisation. The way we currently communicate negates all that. We rely on the passing down of information through the hierarchy of managers or the distribution of a group email to the employees as worthy forms of communication. Unfortunately, this is ineffective and misses out on the context, passion, guidance and energy of leadership. We as human beings rely on energy.

Positive and motivated energy helps bring groups of employees along the journey of performance and achievement towards the vision of the organisation. How can we transfer that energy through levels of management, where some are blockers, and where some managers rely on communicating via electronic media like email?

Web of connectedness...

I started to ponder why communication is so important in high-performing organisations. I came across a poster from Mentally Healthy WA, which had three key words on it: Act, Belong, Commit. In my mind these three words are critical for the health of any organisation. When we feel like we belong to a group, we become committed. When we become committed, we act in the interest of the group. When we act in the interest of the group, our feeling of belonging deepens and our resulting actions are more committed.

My simple view is that open, honest, two-way transparent communication creates the feeling of connectedness or belonging that binds people to a group or organisation. It is probably no different to the web of connectedness that binds us to our family. I believe corporate communication should be the same as the daily conversation at the dinner table. It should operate with the same openness and honesty that is found in our family discussions, disagreements, activities, good times and not so good times – this is what keeps us connected to our family group.

Sense of belonging...

There's a saying that "blood is thicker than water". I guess it means that the bond and commitment between family members is much stronger than the bond between non-family members. Maybe the strength of the bond and commitment between family members stems from the amount of time (years) the cycle of Act, Belong, Commit has had to survive.

Some people mightn't like the idea of me relating organisations to families as there are dysfunctional and unhappy families. Hey, guess what, there are also dysfunctional and unhappy organisations too. It's the fabric of life.

In our Rotary club, it's the regular meetings, conversations, fundraising activities creating a web of connectedness that motivate us to Belong, Act and Commit. When we lose that web of connectedness and we begin to feel that we don't belong anymore, we become discontented, unhappy and we eventually leave the group. Unfortunately, leaving a volunteer group is much easier than leaving a family or an organisation that you work for (although, the number of times our kids have threatened to leave home suggests otherwise!).

At the risk of potentially offending psychology-based HR professionals, I like to use Abraham Maslow's theory on human motivation. (Yes I am aware of the many theories in this area, but I tend to like the simplicity of Maslow's pyramid). Maslow used the terms "physiological", "safety", "belongingness and love", "esteem" and "self-actualisation" to describe the stages of human motivation. Maslow's theory suggests that the most basic level of human need (physiological and safety) must be met before the individual will focus motivation on upper level needs. Once the basic human survival needs are met (food, clothing, wellbeing, shelter, safety, security) the third level in the hierarchy is the need to feel a **sense of belonging** in order to be motivated. According to Maslow, humans need to feel acceptance among their social groups both large and small. This explains why belonging is so important in high-performing groups. The members of our Rotary Club have a strong sense of belonging and consequently are motivated and committed to give up their free time to serve the community.

Engaging communication, along with that connectedness, is the bind or glue that keeps all of us engaged and motivated to belong to an organisation. In the process, we (hopefully) become committed, act with passion, and serve the organisation with loyalty.

Maslow's hierarchy of needs:

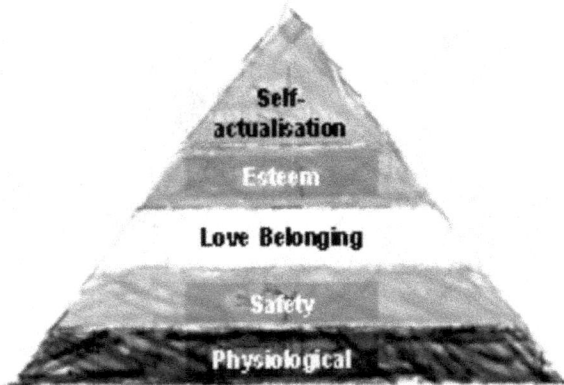

Communication structures...

In my organisations, we have utilised three forms of communication structures that we have found quite effective. The structures consist of:

1.   **Weekly** flat communication
2.   Monthly **team brief** cascade
3.   Six monthly **"state of the nation"** flat communication

Current hierarchical communication structure...

Leadership needs to communicate in an open, honest, transparent way that encourages two-way communication. The problem is that our current hierarchy reporting structure (see Figure 4-1) is not great at downwards and across-the-organisation communication. The current structure (I will term as "hierarchical") is great at collection of data and passing information upwards towards the executive team and CEO. In this structure the CEO is at the pinnacle of the information flow and he or she is likely to be the most informed of all aspects of the organisation.

Figure 4-1 – Typical management reporting structure

I have an analogy that the CEO is the conductor of a symphony orchestra. To co-ordinate the entire organisation he or she needs to be familiar with all parts of the orchestra including percussion, horns, strings, bass, piano and so on.

Similarly, in organisations this conductor-like system is designed for efficient upwards flow of information and communication. You only have to see the extensive reports and spreadsheets that flow up the organisation to know this. Unfortunately, the structure is not great at communication or flow of information down the organisation and definitely not across the organisation between teams and departments. It also tends to involve one-way rather than two-way communication.

The great leaders are like the best conductors - they reach
beyond the notes to reach the magic in the players
Blaine Lee

So why do we complain about "silo mentality" in companies when we actually have communication structures that encourage silos within the workplace? For those of you who are unsure of what I mean by "silo mentality" it is described as employees who only focus on their immediate tasks rather than taking into account the bigger objectives of the group. They don't see sharing of valuable information and helping others as a benefit.

The effective and efficient information flow downwards and sidewards across departments will depend on the openness and communicative motivation of the leader and executive team. We all know how busy they are.

I'm certainly not advocating a change to the normal hierarchal reporting structure of organisations. Instead, I'm suggesting that when we communicate, a flat sharing communication structure (see Figure 4-2) can be very effective in encouraging open, honest, transparent communication across an entire organisation. In the process it can break down the manipulation and stranglehold that managers can have on information flow.

Figure 4-2 – Flat communication structure

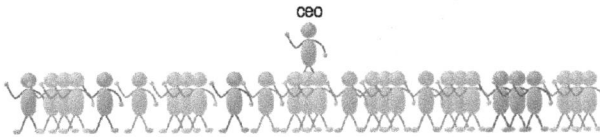

Quarter-time...

I've had much success with this very flat communication structure. Once again, it doesn't matter what type of structure you use as long as it works. I'm sharing an example that worked for me and you should find one that suits your team' requirements and culture. If you look at the above communication structure, it's very similar to a coach addressing players on the football field at quarter time. It's a quick, efficient way to get the same message across to everyone without playing the game of Chinese whispers.

In football you can't afford to have the messages from the coach to the players be distorted or lost in translation. I'm an AFL fan and supporter of the Fremantle Football Club commonly called the "Dockers". Okay, most people reading this book will now want to shut it, but please be kind to us as we haven't won a premiership yet. Like all coaches, our coach Ross Lyon addresses the players in this sort of communication style at the quarter and half-time breaks. And while the team might not have won a premiership, they get closer every year.

This is a good, efficient way to get the bigger game plan to all the players and to make quick, dynamic moves and changes to the team play. It provides the greatest flexibility and nimbleness. It captures the passion and energy of the leader, and everyone sees the whites in Ross Lyon's eyes (and sometimes the fiery red). This is a great direct communication structure, which will cut out the manipulation and control of information and prevent unnecessary games of Chinese whispers. The twist is that in the weekly flat communication structure we get people to brief each other and share information (across departments) rather than the CEO or coach providing the information.

Hook-up...

The weekly meeting is essentially how the flat communication structure works. In an organisation I led, due to our staff being spread out over five countries, the next best thing to face-to-face meetings was a telephone/web conference hook-up. We found a common time when all members of the organisation could join in on the call. As many as 30 or 40 people were on the line including team leaders, managers and key staff. We also invited outside contractors to join the team meeting such as legal, insurance, logistics, or investor relations consultants.

The CEO is the facilitator of the meeting, and according to standard business area topics covered, people were encouraged to quickly and concisely brief the rest of the organisation with their area of business. This could include any achievements, recent activities or challenges facing their department within the business. The CEO, who is just another team member, also reports to the rest of the team on his or her activities for the week.

The first responsibility of a leader is to define reality. The last is to say thank you. In between, the leader is a servant

Max de Pree

Raw information...

Once information is shared with the entire team, no one can manipulate or control it, including the CEO. There's no filter: the information is raw and you have to rely on the maturity of the organisation for it not to be misused. Of course, it requires the right workplace culture for this. You also have to trust your people to manage confidential information, especially if you are a publicly listed company.

This structure allows people to have a good understanding of what other departments do on a weekly basis and encourages working at a wider team level including with outside service providers. The mining person gets to understand what investor relations are doing and vice versa. The accounts department can hear what the marketing and shipping teams are doing and vice versa. The insurance representative gets to understand what the plant people are doing and vice versa. As information is shared from one part of the organisation to all the other sections, employees begin to see the bigger co-ordinated picture and they start to manage the business as a highly-effective group.

As the whole organisation, including service departments, begins to understand the priorities and challenges at hand, everyone begins to help and support each other.

This weekly meeting is where the dynamic target and priority setting takes place for the entire organisation, which replaces the individual KPI system that is used by most organisations. The priority changes week to week and the whole organisation is able to be nimble, flexible and dynamic.

Managers quickly realise that their role is no longer gate-keeper or controller of information; their people know as much as they do. They no longer have control of information anymore. It suddenly dawns on them that their job is not to control information but help their team members succeed in their roles and achieve the overall team objectives. I must admit that when we recruit managers we make sure that they're aware and comfortable with this type of working organisation. We find ego-based managers who are into status, rank and authority don't join us.

The duration of the weekly meeting generally isn't more than 45 minutes. In this short period, the whole organisation gets to know what's going on, saving the need for many side meetings with team leaders or managers repeating the information over and over again. To get the information to the shop floor we encourage attendees to pass on the information to their team members in the same sort of direct, flat communication. They usually get a bullet point summary of what was said and can use it as a briefing reference. Once again, it is not a perfect system but it works well.

Employee comments:
"The CEO created and maintained a very open communication culture and discouraged the 'silo mentality'. He broke the control on flow of information through open weekly meetings and would involve not only all the employees but also external contractors and consultants so that everyone was on the same page"

Anand Sheth (Manager)
Previous employee

Team briefing...

The second communication structure we find quite effective is the monthly (to coincide with monthly results) team briefing cascade system. I experienced this kind of system early in my career and have been using the same system for the last 25 years. It is not important what type of system you use as long as it "touches" everyone in the organisation, right down to the shop floor.

This system utilises the current hierarchical structure to cascade information to all levels of the organisation. The big difference is that information flow is supplemented by local (team) information as it cascades down through the organisation. The other important point is that questions at all levels are recorded and cascaded back up to the CEO for answering at the next team briefing. Usually if someone has a question, other people probably have the same one.

The system helps to provide all staff, whatever level and function, with a clear understanding of results, changes and developments affecting their working lives. Successful team briefing means fewer misunderstandings or rumours within a team, site and the organisation as a whole. It is a two-way process – not just about informing people but listening and responding to questions and concerns and providing answers. It is not meant to replace normal, essential, day-to-day communication between team leader and staff.

How does team briefing work?

The executive team and CEO provide the core brief, which forms the basis for the local briefing meetings each month. Each executive delivers a verbal face-to-face team briefing. Each direct report brief is verbally delivered to their respective teams; as the core brief cascades through each department, additional relevant information at the local level is added. The local brief is prepared by each team's immediate manager and addresses issues which are of direct concern to them. Only a small percentage of the information will be 'core' items passed down from higher up in the organisation. The objective is to brief every individual in the whole organisation right down to the shop floor within 48 hours of the core brief being given.

Typical team briefing template

Core Briefing	Local Briefing
• External changes • Organisational focus • Main priorities • Financial results • Monthly performance • Workplace changes • Challenges next month	• Local changes • Local monthly performance • Social issues • Roster • Personnel movements • Issues to be discussed • Challenges next month
Questions received: 1. When are we getting upgrade on server? 2. Is the planned outage still on in November?	None
Attendance: **Team leader:** J Smith J Citizen, A Employee, B Citizen, A Brown	

I must admit it takes a lot of discipline and commitment to maintain this kind of communication structure. I sometimes struggle with it as well.

"State of the nation" briefings...

The third communication structure that supplements the previous structures is the face-to-face "state of the nation" briefings by the CEO or the leader. This utilises the flat structure once again but this time everyone in the organisation (not just the key people in the weekly structure) is briefed face-to-face once every six months or once every year. If the organisation is larger and widespread this involves a roadshow once a year for the executive.

The idea of this "state of the nation" briefing is for the leader or CEO to articulate the vision of the organisation, vision of the workplace culture and how the group is to meet the challenges ahead. As I mentioned previously, people need to see the passion in a leader's eyes, the enthusiasm in their voice and to feel the energy of their conviction as their head of organisation. Positive and motivated energy helps bring staff along the journey of performance and achievement towards the vision of the organisation. Unfortunately, it does take a lot of time and effort to meet this commitment. You might ask if it is as effective if the leader taped their briefing and distributed it by email to everyone in the organisation. I will let you answer that question yourself.

Emails are not effective...

Many companies today think that email and mobile phone communication can help solve their communication problems, but they can't. Team briefing works because it's face-to-face and between the employees' immediate manager (generally most trusted), which is essential for all types of communication, including sensitive.

How many of us have received an email from a colleague who is seated less than a metre away, asking a simple question that can be answered in under 10 seconds in person? What about those long chain emails within your own team that become impossible to follow, when it would have been easier to just have a face-to-face discussion in a meeting room?

An Australian advertising company, Atomic 212, made the decision to ban internal emails. The company's CEO Jason Dooris, with over 20 years' experience in the industry, said, *"I don't think the industry is as good as it used to be and I don't think people enjoy their jobs as much. They're not learning as much as well"*. Dooris blames this on the constant dependence on emails, which is affecting companies across most verticals.

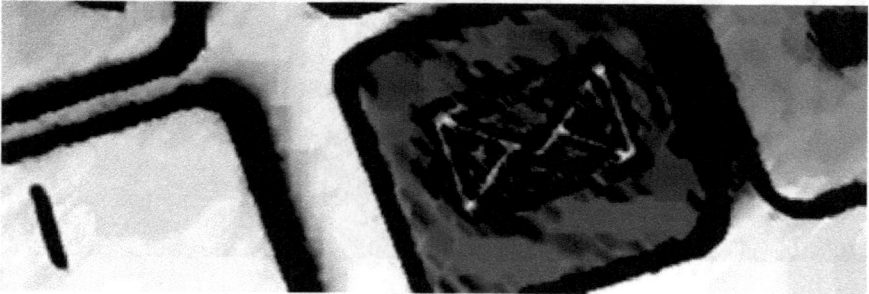

Most of Dooris' company's 50-person staff had never known a world without email so it was a bold and risky move to ban it across the entire organisation but he was adamant that it would be beneficial. *"When people start to familiarise themselves with doing things without email, everything just fell into place"*, he said.

"Employees who believe that management is concerned about them as a whole person - not just an employee - are more productive, more satisfied, more fulfilled. Satisfied employees mean satisfied customers, which leads to profitability"

Anne M. Mulcahy

Productivity, believe it or not, actually went up as a result of the internal email ban by Atomic's CEO. While the company is still tracking the progress of the move, Dooris estimated a 38-42% increase in productivity based on the key deliverables such as the time it takes for staff to perform certain tasks for clients and in the office. *"I genuinely believe, having seen what I've seen, that this is the next wave of change in workplace communication"*, he said.

In a nutshell...

Constant, open, honest and transparent communication is hard work and the benefits and results are not often immediately obvious. In my simplistic view, that hard work is essential in creating the feeling of connectedness or belonging that binds people within a group or organisation. We need that web of connectedness in order to become a high-performing organisation.

Chapter 5
What really motivates people?

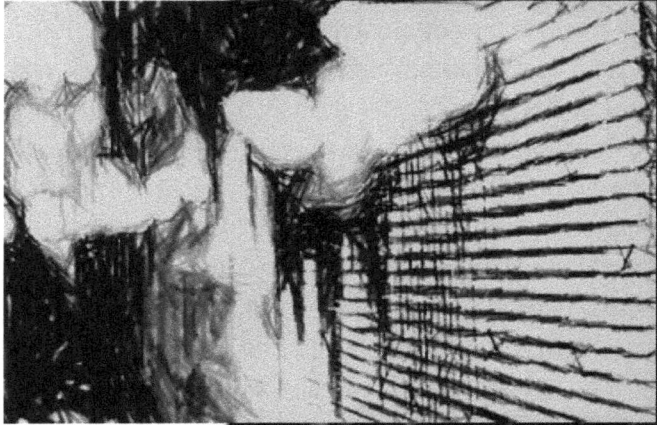

What really motivates people?

Now let's examine the question of what motivates an employee. It could be said that this question is at the heart of modern management. Are employees motivated by objectives or goals, or are they likely to try harder if offered financial rewards or incentives?

Are we motivated by objectives?

Most of us were taught in management school: goals and objectives motivate people. The system of Management by Objectives (MBO) was first popularised by Peter Drucker in his 1954 book The Practice of Management. MBO is a process of identifying objectives that management and employees agree on and understand what they need to do within the organisation in order to achieve them. Incentives (in the form of monetary bonuses) are often linked to results in reaching the objectives. This forms the basis of how we manage and motivate our people. The principle of MBO is for employees to have a clear understanding of their roles and the responsibilities expected of them.

Are we motivated by financial incentives?

Or does extra financial rewards or incentives (the extra pocket money allowance or the extra scoop of ice cream in my family example) motivate people? Assuming that people are properly and fairly remunerated for their work, skills and experience according to market conditions, is the extra financial incentive a strong motivating factor?

We, as managers, have been programmed to rely upon the "carrot and stick" approach. If you do something well then you'll be rewarded with a carrot, and if you do something undesirable then you'll be punished with a stick. We believe, just like laboratory mice or Pavlov's dog (his name rings a bell), that we all respond to simple stimuli and responses. People, are motivated by carrots, right?

Top 10 job satisfaction motivators...

Many studies have looked at what motivates employees and what produces high job satisfaction levels. Typical results from these studies are shown in Table 5-1.

Table 5-1 – Typical top 10 job satisfaction motivators

1. Achievement
2. Learning
3. Inspiration
4. Creativity
5. Fun and enjoyment
6. Improvement
7. Financial rewards
8. Change and variety
9. Identity and purpose
10. Stability

What is interesting from these surveys is that objectives and KPIs (key performance indicators) don't show up in the top 10 motivators; and financial rewards is at the bottom end of the list, in fact, number seven on the list. Surprised?

These results are typical of the workplace today. Financial rewards are not a high motivator nor job satisfaction factor for employees and yet we rely on them as our number one motivating tool!

Warm fuzzies please...

On the top of the motivator list are things like achievement, learning, inspiration, creativity, fun and enjoyment. I describe these grey motivators as "warm fuzzies": they give people a nice, warm and fuzzy feeling. The "warm fuzzies" happen to relate very closely to the web of connectedness and sense of belonging I mentioned in the previous chapter. They belong to the emotional side of employees.

For logic-based managers this is a real problem as these motivators are very grey and nebulous. *"How the hell do I inspire my people? How do I create achievement and learning in the workplace? How do I create creativity for someone doing payroll, for example? Give me something clear, concrete and logical that I can implement and not have to worry about."*

We all know that an inspired employee gives his or her all to the organisation and constantly strives to be and do their best. Inspired employees use their skills and talents to their full potential.

When you are inspired by some great purpose, some extraordinary project, all your thoughts break their bonds: your mind transcends limitations, your consciousness expands in every direction, and you find yourself in a new, great, and wonderful world.
Patanjali – Author of Yoga Sutra 184 AD

If you still don't believe that financial rewards have little bearing on motivation, then just have a look at sporting teams, or volunteer, non-profit and non-private groups. There are many motivated people within these organisations who are not driven by financial rewards. What makes someone train two or three times a week and then play on the weekends in an amateur sporting team? What makes someone devote their valuable time to helping others and still stay motivated and loyal to the cause when there are no monetary rewards?

What motivated your primary school teacher to inspire and educate you far beyond the call of duty? What about the Olympic athletes who dedicate their lives to their chosen sport to pursue their dreams? And what drives musicians or artists: financial rewards and incentives?

Purpose and passion...

Camille Preston, founder of AIM Leadership, writing for Fortune 500 in 2015 said "knowing the why" was what drove managers and employees. She advocates asking oneself, "why is this task or project important and who does it impact?"; by adding passion to the purpose – by having emotion drive the motion – bosses and employees alike can shift their energy from having to do something to wanting to.

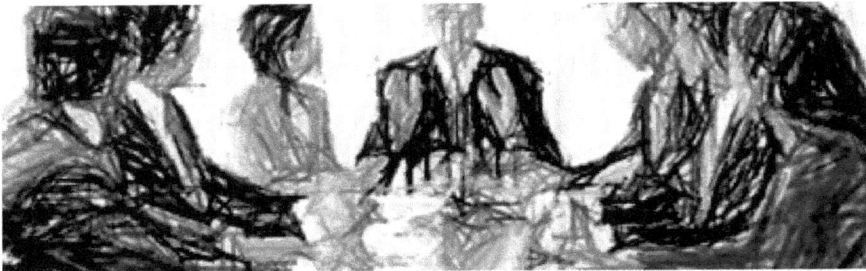

Preston discusses results from a study of employees, all of whom derive meaning and significance from their work; the employees were three times more likely to stay with their organisation; these employees had 1.7 times higher job satisfaction, and were 1.4 times more engaged at work.

Erica Dhawan, a researcher at Harvard's Centre for Public Leadership, explains how feedback is another great motivator for employees. She recommends employees to seek feedback on how they're going at work; if someone can see the difference their efforts are making it pushes them to achieve more, according to Dhawan.

Individual KPIs...

Based on my own practical experience, I started to challenge the idea that employees are motivated by individual objectives or goals. I challenged the formal process of setting individual key performance indicators at the start of every year and then monitoring and evaluating at the end of the period. I disagree with linking any financial incentive with these individual key performance indicators or objectives.

As soon as these key performance indicators and objectives are set, situations often change within the organisation and the KPIs may no longer be relevant. The employee is now in a dilemma of chasing the formal KPIs, which have some financial impact, or pursuing new, more appropriate targets that have greater benefit to the company. In addition, employees might be prone to distort results, falsely representing the achievement of targets that were set in a short-term or narrow fashion.

Ban individual KPIs...

In our organisations, we've banned individual objectives and KPIs. We don't waste our time setting them formally, then monitoring or evaluating them. We have no financial incentives linked to them at all. They serve no purpose except to drive the idea of individual self-centred thinking.

If you're trying to create a culture of teamwork where everyone is working efficiently by helping each other to achieve the overall team outcomes, why implement a system that encourages competition via the "looking good" theory? *"Do I really care about the rest of the team as long as I meet my individual KPIs?"*

Do we believe in targets at all? Yes, of course but they have to be informal, dynamic team targets, common to all, that change and flex with changes in the company. The targets for the whole organisation should be communicated regularly and reinforced during the weekly team meetings. This is the way to keep the organisation nimble and dynamic.

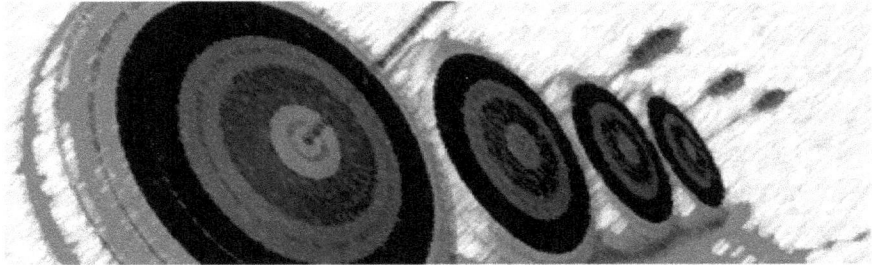

I remember when the management team of one of my operations was concerned that we didn't have individual KPIs for all the staff. The group approached me at a big management dinner and asserted that individual KPIs were the fundamental basis of management. I got up and addressed the entire team. I said that under pressure I was now going to give an individual KPI to a member of the management group. I picked John, the safety manager.

"John, your KPI is for the site to have no lost time and be injury free for the next 12 months." I then asked my audience if that was a good KPI, and they all nodded in agreement. I then asked John how he felt now that he had been given a KPI. He replied, *"no different"*. *"What? Why no different John? The theory says that now you have an objective or KPI you should be more motivated and more committed"*, I said. John responded wisely, *"I feel no different because I already knew what I had to do."*

When you have engaged and motivated employees, they know what they need to achieve

Our job as managers is to keep staff engaged, motivated and connected, which will eventually result in truly outstanding team performance.

What about financial incentives?

Being from the private sector I'm not advocating banning financial rewards or incentive systems. What I'm saying is that we shouldn't rely on such rewards as our primary motivating tool. In our organisations, we have a once-a-year bonus system, subject to the whole team achieving several key targets. We also have a long-term incentive system with the issue of performance shares. Once again, this is subject to overall team outcomes. I consider this financial rewards system as a competitive requirement in the marketplace. They're nice to have if we all work as a team and achieve great things together but I don't consider them a motivating tool.

> *An employee's motivation is a direct result of the sum of interactions with his or her manager.*
>
> Bob Nelson

What motivates people are people: managers and leaders who focus on the "warm fuzzies" to inspire their staff and in the process build a kind, compassionate and happy place in which to work.

What makes employees quit?

In a recent study about why employees resign it was found that the immediate boss or supervisor is an overriding factor. The study reveals nine errors made by bosses/supervisors that result in valuable employees resigning:

1. they overwork good people
2. they don't recognise contribution
3. they don't care about employees
4. they don't honour their commitments
5. they hire or promote the wrong people

6. they don't let people pursue passions
7. they don't develop people's skills
8. they fail to engage employees' creativity
9. they fail to challenge people intellectually

As you can see from the above list, the many reasons relate to the "warm fuzzies" of what motivates people and provides job satisfaction.

Honour their commitments…

Most of the issues listed on the previous list are self-explanatory, but I do want to comment on number four: 'they don't honour their commitments'. In all my management years, this is the single-most common issue in our organisations today causing employees to resign. Time after time, I come across employees that are so upset and dissatisfied with their organisation because their supervisors made them a promise or commitment and did not honour it. I understand that these supervisors have all the great intentions and are genuine when making commitments to their staff.

There are many reasons why this can happen in an organisation, often they are beyond a manager's control. Like life, our workplace environment is in a constant state of flux; plans change and promises can't always be kept. For example, a manager's commitment to his employee did not eventuate as it was not approved by upper management. This is a typical occurrence in the workplace today. Someone is awarded a job or a promotion and the pay rate is kept down until a follow-up review is conducted further down the track. "We will set it at this rate and in six months we will review the rate, depending on how you go." Sure as hell, the salary is never reviewed and no adjustment is ever made. Maybe the manager moves on and the employee spends the rest of the time being disgruntled. I once asked a guy why he never spoke up and his reply was that he shouldn't have to remind anyone of a commitment made by management. He remained suspicious and disgruntled about management regardless of their good intentions.

Another scenario, "we will seriously look at getting you a promotion in the next 12 months." This often fails to happen and the employee feels that something was promised and never delivered.

The only advice I would give managers is to NEVER promise anything; don't put yourself in the position where you have to use your word to try and make something right. As in the pay rate example, allocate the employee the correct salary rate upfront. In the promotion example, implement action to make the promotion happen without any prior verbal commitment. You're better off delivering the good news, rather than promising it.

> **Employee comments:**
> "Providing the environment for employees to have some ownership and self-achievement is a fantastic motivation that allows most employees to want to come to work and achieve something, feel part of the team, not just a number stuck in a box with no room to exercise their thoughts and contribute in many ways. Most people always wish to do the right thing, want to contribute and achieve. With a sense of autonomy and being able to work and achieve without close supervision and with trust, employees consider this to be very important, hence the job satisfaction is not so much just based on salary. To be happy at work is the most valuable element for employees."
>
> Roger Pover (Manager)
> Previous employee

In a nutshell...
Setting individual objectives or key performance indicators, monitoring them and evaluating them, is a waste of time and resources. The KPI system serves little purpose except to drive a competitive environment and discourage a culture of teamwork. Why implement a system that encourages competition by trying to "look good"? What motivates people is people.

Chapter 6
Job descriptions
are blueprints for silos

Job descriptions are blueprints for silos

A job description is exactly that, a description of the general tasks, functions and responsibilities of a position within an organisation. It also identifies the person for that position to report to and may include qualifications and skills required for the job.

In some companies the job description is reviewed during performance appraisal time to see if the employee has met their role's responsibilities and accountabilities. During the recruitment process a job description is great for conveying to a prospective candidate what the job entails. It is ideal to communicate and match the qualifications and skills of candidates.

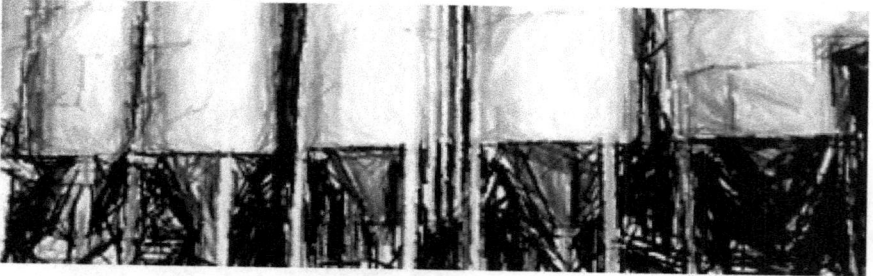

Let's build silos...

Unfortunately, job descriptions have become blueprints for silos. How often have you heard someone say "that is not in my job description", or, "if you want me to do those extra tasks, you need to change my job description". As you know, the silo mentality is when groups do not openly share information or knowledge with other groups in the same company. This kind of silo thinking reduces efficiency, morale and stems from a competitive corporate culture.

A recent Forbes article, 'The Silo Mentality: How To Break Down The Barriers' blames top management and conflicted leadership teams (culture) for silos in an organisation. *"This competitive culture leads to long term harm to the organisation.*

as a whole by creating resentment and cynicism within the teams." The Forbes article recommends creating a unified vision and working towards a common goal as ways to break down the silo mentality.

Throw job descriptions out...

In our organisations we don't feel the need to clarify and review an employee's job description or responsibilities. We believe that by doing so encourages people to think that their job and duties are fixed and defined rather than flexible and dynamic. We encourage our employees to do "whatever it takes" to help others in order for the team to achieve its overall goals. Why should it matter that someone goes beyond their perceived role and makes the extra effort to help a colleague? In the end, that's what teamwork is all about.

We find that when we have the right culture, helping each other all happens naturally and without fuss.

We have "whatever it takes" job descriptions

Blame game...

Job descriptions are essentially aimed at clarifying roles, responsibilities and accountabilities of employees. Yves Morieux (Boston Consulting Group), in a Ted Talk presentation ("How too many rules at work keep you from getting things done") says that organisations are constantly trying to put accountability in someone else's hands. This clear line of accountability is fundamentally so that we know who to blame when something goes wrong.

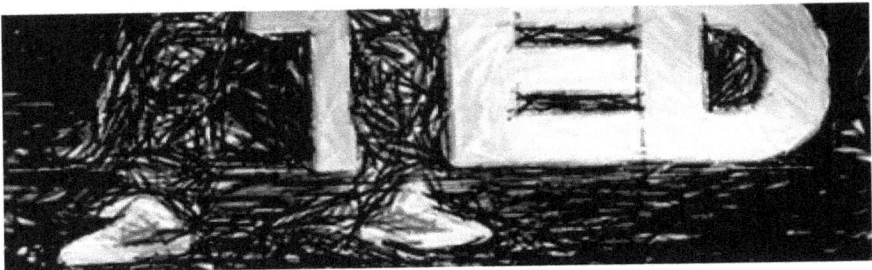

"We pay more attention on knowing who to blame in case we fail than creating the conditions to succeed. Don't go for clarity go for fussiness. Fussiness overlaps." Morieux shows in this insightful talk that too often an overload of rules, processes and metrics keeps us from doing our best work together.

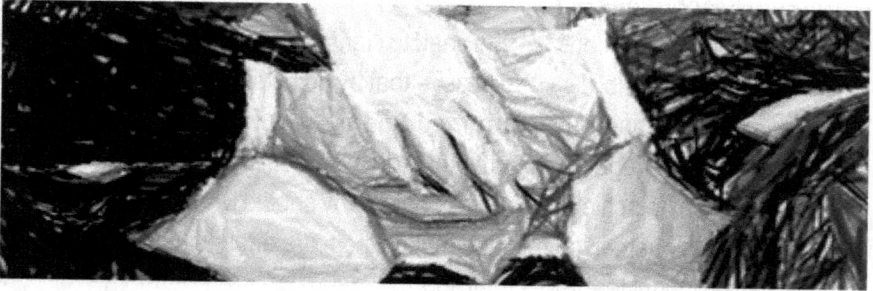

Break down the silos, co-operate...

Becoming focused on very-defined roles, responsibilities and accountabilities and then rewarding individuals that keep within their defined boxes discourages co-operation and teamwork. We have accidentally built workplace cultures that discourage our employees to go beyond their pre-determined boxes, co-operate and help one another. We need to create organisations in which it becomes individually useful for people to co-operate.

Morieux argues that co-operation still means that the whole is worth more than the sum of the parts. He states that there is a miracle of co-operation. It multiplies energy, intelligence, and human effort, rather than individual performances. *"We should be focused on how we work together and how each effort contributes to the effort of others."*

In a nutshell...

Job descriptions have become blueprints for building silos. We have accidentally built workplace cultures that discourage our employees to go beyond their roles, co-operate and help one another. We need to create organisations in which it becomes individually useful for people to co-operate and where they are rewarded for doing so.

Chapter 7
Ban the exit interview

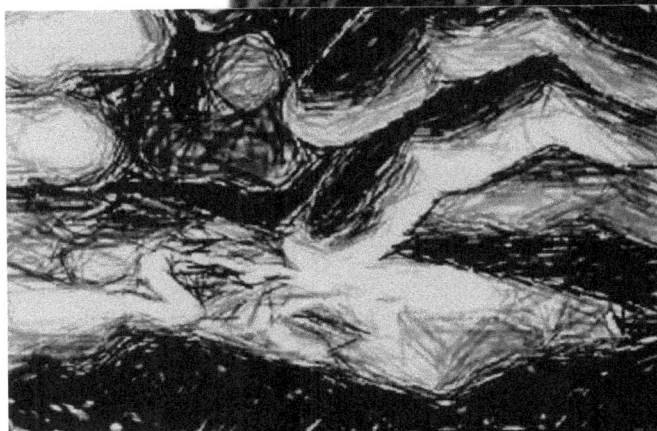

Ban the exit interview

As you know, an exit interview is a survey conducted with an employee leaving an organisation; usually a middle or larger-sized company. The idea is that the information gained from the interview can be used to improve the organisation and reduce general employee turnover.

We all accept that turnover and unhappy staff that are often absent can be costly for business. Recruiting and hiring are also expensive processes. Very unhappy staff may also litigate against the company. So it's in an organisation's best interest to find out why their employee is leaving. Exit interviews are usually conducted by a company's HR department either just before or soon after an employee departs to ensure the employee's reasons for leaving are fresh in their mind. Common questions during the exit interview address the reasons for leaving, job satisfaction, frustrations, and feedback concerning company policies or procedures. Questions may relate to the work environment, supervisors, compensation, the work itself, or the company culture. Some typical exit interview questions may include:

> What are your main reasons for leaving?
> What did you like most/least about the organisation?
> Did you have enough resources and support to do your job?
> What, if improved, might have made you think about staying?
> Would you recommend the organisation to others as a good
> place to work/study/join?

The results of the exit interview are collated and generally distributed to the key managers. The results are usually treated confidentially with a limited distribution.

Way too late...

I think these questions are very important and they have the potential to gauge and monitor the health of the workplace culture. Unfortunately, though, such interviews often take place way too late – it's a case of shutting the barn door after the horse has bolted.

And they're usually directed at the wrong set of employees. Shouldn't managers be asking the same questions and getting feedback from the employees currently working in the organisation (before they leave)?

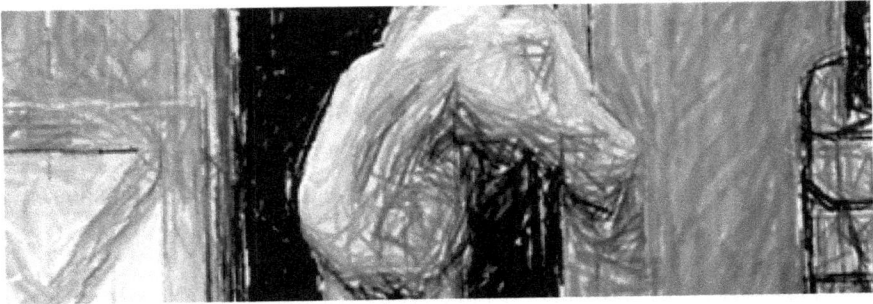

Shouldn't they be asking current employees about their job satisfaction and frustrations and seeking feedback concerning company policies or procedures before the employees get so upset they throw in the towel?

Shouldn't managers be asking current staff about their work environment, supervisors, compensation, the work itself, and the company culture? I'd have thought that by talking to staff way before they get so fed up they leave, a manager could have done something about a problem before it became serious and affected morale and turnover. Shouldn't the workplace culture be for the employee to take responsibility and speak up in the first place?

Arguably, the whole concept of exit interviews is flawed and a complete waste of time. In my experience, the results and feedback are often dismissed by senior management anyway and any meaningful changes or improvement to the organisation are rare. So why do them in the first place?

Exit interviews are a retrospective management tool rather than a proactive forward-looking indicator of the health of the organisation. When employees start to leave then high turnover becomes a major problem; it is way too late as culture becomes entrenched and it is very difficult to turn around.

The entrance strategy is actually
more important than the exit strategy.

Edward Lampert

Love and marriage...

Marriage is a good analogy. If a relationship starts to feel a bit shaky, isn't it best to talk to your spouse before the marriage breaks down and the whole family suffers a painful divorce? It's too late after the split to find out from your ex what went wrong and how the relationship could have been improved. I'm sure you'd agree that it's best to constantly monitor satisfaction levels (my wife constantly tells me anyway) in an ongoing relationship rather than find out as he or she is storming out the door with their cases packed.

There's a trick to the graceful exit. It begins with the vision to recognise
when a job, a life stage, a relationship is over - and to let go.
It means leaving what's over without denying its value.

Ellen Goodman

We've banned exit interviews...

In our organisations, we have banned exit interviews. Our poor HR manager (yes we do have one) also enjoys not having to conduct them. So how do we monitor the health of the organisation and workplace culture? It really doesn't matter what feedback tool you use but use one. There are many options out there in the management world, but in our organisations we use standard employee satisfaction surveys (see next chapter) to gain feedback and measure employee engagement, morale and performance.

Say goodbye properly...

When an employee leaves a workplace on good terms, with many years of loyal and dedicated service, there is often no formal acknowledgement or "thank you" from the organisation. It is often left to the employee's local team to organise a morning tea (often at the expense of colleagues) and pitch together to purchase a small "goodbye" gift. The responsibility of acknowledging and bidding a proper farewell to these loyal but departing employees lies squarely with the organisation. Provide a gift of appreciation and say goodbye according to the values of the workplace.

Early in my career, the company I worked for had a small allocation of funds for employees leaving. It was very nice and rewarding for a token of appreciation to be received for the loyal years of service. The gesture was always valued by the entire workforce. Departing employees are the ambassadors of your company or organisation. In our organisation, we often provided a framed photo memento of the site they worked at, and that was really appreciated by those departing employees. Just a simple but powerful gesture!

Saying hello (again)...

I remember a situation in the early part of my management career at the plant level. A maintenance manager with five years' service at the site resigned to take on another job opportunity. A promotion, I guessed, and we were all glad for him. We provided a farewell dinner and as a token of our appreciation we gave him a small gift as well as a framed photo of the site as a memento of his time with us. He left us and started his new job with enthusiasm. About two months later, he visited us and asked for his old job back (the vacant position had not been filled at that stage). There was a management meeting and we had to decide if we would give him back his old job. What would you have done in this situation?

We gave him back his old job against corporate advice and he stayed at the site providing another 10 years of loyal, outstanding service. I guess sometimes people need to see "what is on the other side" to appreciate what they have.

In a nutshell...

The traditional exit interview with a departing employee is a waste of time and way too late. Exit interviews are a retrospective management tool rather than a proactive forward-looking indicator of the health of the organisation. The questions are, however, very important and should be directed to employees before they leave the organisation. It is also important for organisations to acknowledge and say goodbye properly to departing employees as they are the future ambassadors of your organisation.

Chapter 8
Take a health check

Take a health check

So, how do we monitor the health of the organisation and workplace culture? It doesn't matter what kind of survey tool you use or the questions you ask, the fact that you are asking your employees how they feel is the most important thing. The process of engagement is the process of feeling that management cares and wants to do something about it. Yes it is that simple.

In our organisations we use standard employee satisfaction surveys to gain feedback in order to measure employee engagement, morale and performance. Answered anonymously, these surveys are usually conducted every six months. The results enable management to find out how staff feel about aspects of their employment such as working conditions or motivation. The surveys provide insight that regular channels of communication may not. The team inventory survey I've used in my last 20 years as a manager comes from Hoevemeyer (1993).

We ask our staff to respond to the following statements:

1. Everyone on my team knows exactly why we do what we do.
2. The team leader consistently lets the team members know how we are doing on meeting our customer's expectations.
3. Everyone on my team has a significant amount of say or influence on decisions that affect their job.

4. If outsiders were to describe the way we communicate within our team, they would use words such as "open", "honest, "timely" and "two-way".
5. Team members have the skills they need to accomplish their role within the team.
6. Everyone on the team knows and understands the team's priorities.
7. As a team, we work together to set clear, achievable and appropriate goals.
8. I would rather have the team decide how to do something than have the team leader give step-by-step instructions.
9. As a team, we are able to work together to solve potentially destructive conflicts rather than ignoring conflicts.
10. The role each member of the team is expected to play makes sense to the whole team.
11. The team understands how it fits into the organisation.
12. If my team does not reach a goal, I am more interested in finding out why we have failed to meet the goal than I am in reprimanding the team members.

13. The team has so much ownership of the work that, if necessary, we would offer to stay late to finish a job.
14. The team leader encourages every person on the team to be open and honest, even if people have to share information that goes against what the team leader would.
15. There is a good match between the capabilities and responsibilities of each person on the team.

16. Everyone on the team is working towards accomplishing the same thing.
17. The team has the support and resources it needs to meet customer expectations.
18. The team knows as much about what is going on in the organisation as the team leader does, because the team leader always keeps everyone up-to-date.
19. The team leader believes that everyone on the team has something to contribute – such as knowledge, skills and information – that is of value to all.
20. Team members clearly understand the team's unwritten rules of how to behave within the group.

Respondents indicate their attitudes by checking how strongly they agree or disagree with the statements; the employee gives a rating from 1 to 5, from "strongly disagree" to "strongly agree".

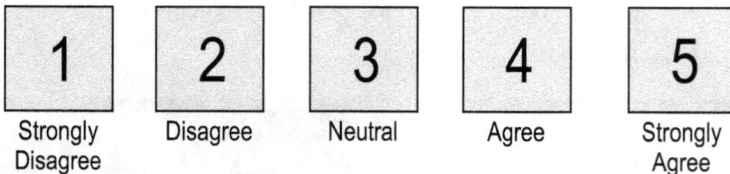

1	2	3	4	5
Strongly Disagree	Disagree	Neutral	Agree	Strongly Agree

Because we focus on teamwork and team outcomes, all the questions centre on team effectiveness. This reinforces the idea that an individual has to take ownership of their team and how it operates. It empowers each team member to consider workplace conditions, communication, happiness and job satisfaction.

The most effective teams are those that excel in all five areas:

1. *Team mission* (Q1, 5, 10, 15): each person on the team should know exactly why the team exists and what it contributes to the organisation.

2. *Goal achievement* (Q2, 6, 11, 16): team members should be committed to establishing team goals, measuring progress toward them, and attaining them.
3. *Empowerment* (Q3, 7, 12, 17): in an empowered environment each person on the team has confidence in the team's ability to achieve its mission. They have the authority, the responsibility and the accountability they need to get their job done.
4. *Communication* (Q4, 8, 13, 18): everyone on the team must be able to communicate openly and honestly with each other without being afraid to be explicit.
5. *Positive roles and norms* (Q5, 9, 14, 19): effective teams assign work based on the strengths of each team member, even if that work is not in their job description. The norms (rules of behaviour) need to be positive and to contribute to the goals and missions of the team.

Warts and all...

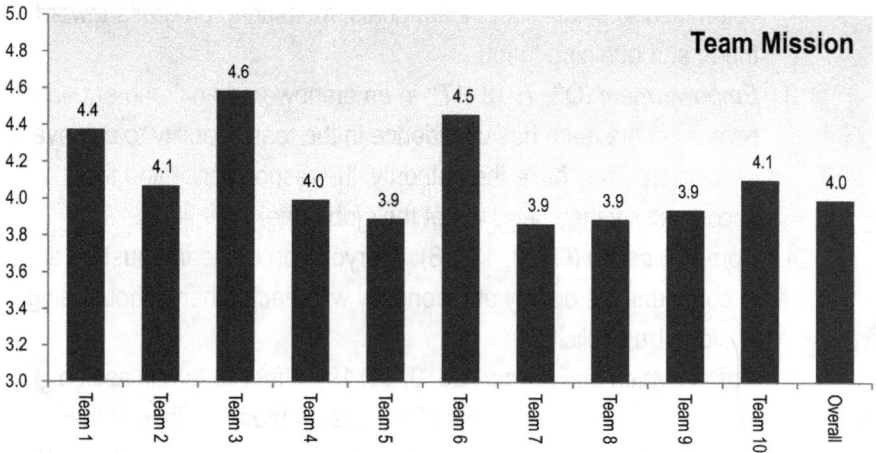

Team Mission

In our organisations we publish the results for every employee to see rather than use the results as a confidential tool for senior management. It's an open, honest and transparent approach. Everyone gets to see the individual team results in its raw form, warts and all.

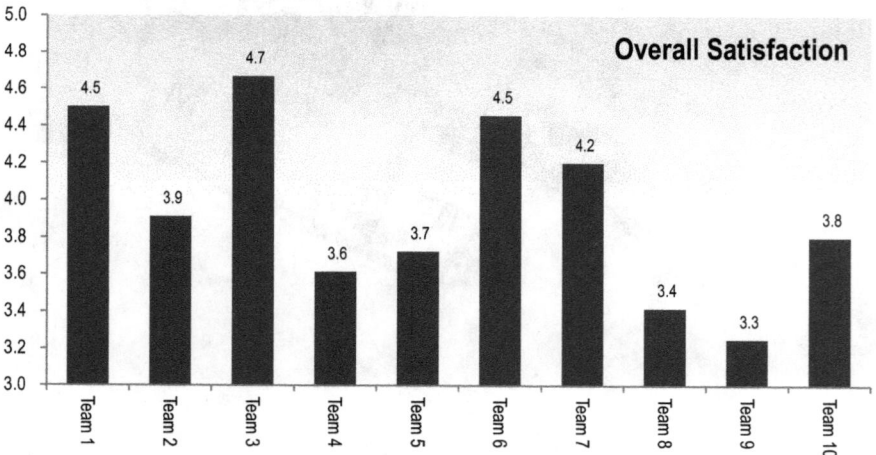

Overall Satisfaction

Let the teams sort it out for themselves...

There is a strong temptation for management to intervene based on the survey data. Someone in head office might wonder why overall satisfaction scores from team 9 (see previous page) were down and ask the manager to prepare a report on what improvements they plan to make to improve them. Wrong. Let the team sort it out for themselves.

Effective teams result in employees taking control of their jobs and doing what needs to be done. When you have motivated and engaged employees, people want to improve and they'll therefore find their own solutions. So by just publishing the results and trusting the process, we find that over time, these results improve. Yes, simple as that. As seen in the following graphs, the six monthly results for both communication and teamwork show an improvement over three years for the organisation.

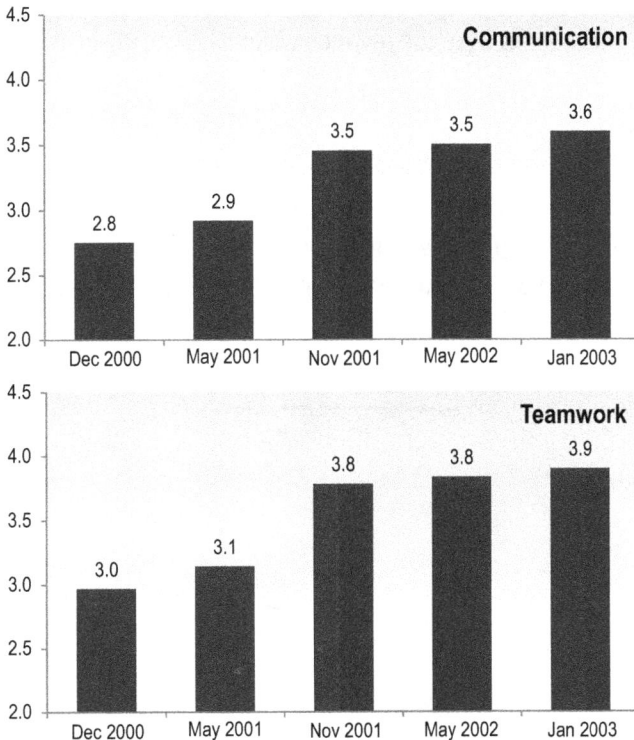

Communication

Date	Score
Dec 2000	2.8
May 2001	2.9
Nov 2001	3.5
May 2002	3.5
Jan 2003	3.6

Teamwork

Date	Score
Dec 2000	3.0
May 2001	3.1
Nov 2001	3.8
May 2002	3.8
Jan 2003	3.9

Effective teams...

Team effectiveness is important in that it frees the manager or facilitator from being involved in the day-to-day details of the group's work. Hoevemeyer says that in comparison with employees, who work individually, effective teams tend to have higher morale, productivity, and greater pride in the job and company. *"They understand the value of working together rather than against each other."*

More hands on deck...

In an Australian Institute of Business blog, the institute's social media co-ordinator Laura Hutton wrote that teamwork at work has many benefits including having more hands on deck. According to Hutton, teams foster the sharing of responsibilities and, because they're made up of people from different backgrounds and levels of experience, offer learning opportunities and the confidence to try more creative options for getting the work done. From a management perspective, she suggests, teams enable companies to take on more work, thus generating extra revenue without having to hire more staff.

In a nutshell...

Gauge the health of your organisation by using employee surveys on a regular basis to measure employee engagement, morale and performance. Openly share the results with every employee and let the teams sort it out for themselves. When you have motivated and engaged employees, and when you trust in the process, we find that over time, these results improve.

Chapter 9
Mission to Mars and back

Mission to Mars and back

So now let me indulge in a hobby horse of mine: the mission statement. Mostly every company has one and they're now spreading to universities, non-profit organisations and other groups. It's commonly understood that a mission statement is designed to communicate the purpose of the organisation. Mission statements are normally short and simple, outlining the organisation's objectives, which are related to the specific sector in which the organisation operates.

It's accepted that properly crafted mission statements serve as filters to separate what is important from what is not: they clearly state which markets will be served and how, and communicate a sense of intended direction to the entire organisation. All sounds pretty sensible, right?

Agonising and arguing...

I was a part of an executive management team of a large Australian mining company, following a merger of two similar companies. A three-day "mission statement" workshop (like going to Mars) was organised, for which managers were flown in from around the globe. We stayed in a golf resort just outside of Perth and the workshop was facilitated by very expensive consultants. There would have been at least 35 key people present and we all wore corporate polo shirts printed specially for the occasion.

The workshop started with introductions and an assessment of the environmental and business factors. We then went onto redefine our target markets, discuss our products' differences from those of our competitors, and talk out our defining characteristics.

We articulated again why we were in business and brainstormed our goals and aspirations as an organisation. Then we agonised and argued (for half a day) about each and every word that appeared in the mission statement. Finally, we made sure we'd covered all the bases: shareholder return, stakeholders, employees, markets, products, environment, safety, profits, growth, ethical conduct, teamwork and so on.

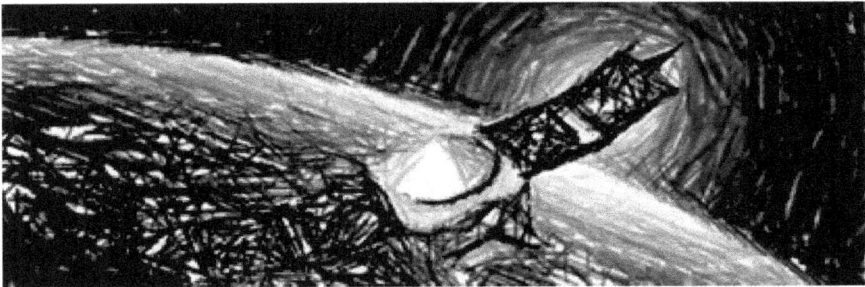

An aspect of mission statement theory is that a statement should guide the actions of the organisation, spell out its overall goal, provide a path, and guide decision-making. The theory is that a statement should provide the framework or context within which the company's strategies are formulated.

In the end, after three long days we came up with what we thought was a great and dynamic mission statement. I'd studied the importance of mission statements in my MBA course and was therefore very excited by this outcome. The next step was to launch and communicate it to all the employees. A mission statement "distils the heart and soul of a company in an engaging, memorable paragraph or two", which we thought we'd achieved.

You learn from your people...

When I took the mission statement to most of the 800 employees who came under my business unit, everyone said that it looked good, but I saw the truth in their eyes. "You guys spent three days in a workshop with all those extra costs to come up with a statement like that? What does it mean anyway? It makes absolutely no difference to my working life".

It was at that point I realised how stupid the mission statement is; the workshop was a complete waste of time. I realised the employees already knew the essence of the business and just because they couldn't recite the mission statement with all its management jargon didn't mean they were unaware of what our purpose was all about. We underestimate our people!

I want to remind you that the mission statement is exactly the same as the published values discussed in Chapter 1. It's a wish list and the true mission of the organisation is in its behaviours and actions. And to think, too, that the market doesn't know what your company or organisation does is also totally ludicrous. What is the use of a stupid statement that actually reads the same for almost every company but is only trying to say it in a different way?

Some examples of silly mission statements:

"We are a market-focused, process-centred organisation that develops and delivers innovative solutions to our customers, consistently out performs our peers, produces predictable earnings for our shareholders, and provides a dynamic and challenging environment for our employees."

"[The company] is a results-orientated oil and gas company that builds value for its shareholders through its employees by creating an atmosphere of optimism, teamwork, creativity, resourcefulness and by dealing with everyone in an open and ethical manner."

"[The company] is committed to supplying the consumer and our customers with the finest, high-quality products and to leading the industry in nutrition research and education. [The company] supports these goals with a corporate philosophy of adhering to the highest ethical conduct in all its business dealings, treatment of its employees, and social and environmental policies."

"Our [company's] goal is to be the most respected global financial services company. Like any other public company, we're obligated to deliver profits and growth to our shareholders. Of equal importance is to deliver those profits and generate growth responsibly."

Where's the passion?...

I'm sure after reading these examples your eyes have started to glaze over and it all starts to seem totally meaningless, right? The mission statements all sound like they were spewed out from a mass mission statement generator. There is no sense of passion, enthusiasm or persuasion in these statements. French philosopher Denis Diderot once said, *"only passions, great passions, can elevate the soul to great things".*

During her study on passion, Pace University professor Melissa Cardon found that passion plays a critical role in an entrepreneur's success. For one thing, passion mobilises a person's energy and enhances one's commitment to a goal. But passion does so much more. According to Cardon, *"Entrepreneurial passion catalyses full blown emotional experiences, complete with engagement of brain and body responses."*

So in our organisations, we have banned mission statements as they serve no purpose whatsoever. Just because almost every top 500 company has one and displays the statement in just about every publication, doesn't mean much, and arguably it's of very little benefit.

So what about a vision?

On the other hand, I believe a vision is quite different. According to Business News Daily a mission statement tells people why your business exists, whereas a vision talks about where your company is heading.

I agree that a vision statement is forward-looking and action-based as it gathers the momentum of the organisation. A simple, powerful vision unifies the organisation's common purpose and direction.

If you are after one, don't spend money on consultants to generate one. Use your heart, feeling and purpose to generate it. Create passion, enthusiasm and emotion in your organisation. Don't labour over it. It should encapsulate the first thing that comes to your mind if someone asks where your organisation is heading. Try to avoid overused buzzwords and clichés. These words are empty, meaningless and used so often they've lost the punch they once had.

Nothing great has ever been achieved without enthusiasm.

Ralph Waldo Emerson

Business school professors at the University of Minnesota found that *"individuals who are rated high on charisma tend to express more positive emotions in their written and spoken communications. Positive emotions include passion, enthusiasm, excitement and optimism."* Further, positive leaders were perceived as more effective and therefore more likely to persuade their followers to do what they want their followers to do.

A great example of a powerful vision is Apple's in 1980: *"To make a contribution to the world by making tools for the mind that advance humankind."*

Also, Save the Children Foundation': *"Our vision is a world in which every child attains the right to survival, protection, development and participation."*

Only needs to be simple but powerful, as per the Make-A-Wish Foundation: *"Our vision is that people everywhere will share the power of a wish."*

Vision for workplace culture...

As far as I'm aware there are not many organisations that have a vision or a vision statement expressing what they are trying to achieve in terms of workplace culture. If a vision statement is a forward-looking, action-focused statement that unifies the common purpose and direction of people, why wouldn't you articulate the vision of workplace culture?

Vision is the art of seeing what is invisible to others.

Jonathan Swift

This is how I articulate the vision to staff at our organisations:
"Imagine that one day you're retired and sitting on a beautiful beach somewhere. You reflect on your working life and you realise that this was the best company and the best place you ever worked at. To make this the best place you ever worked, I need your help to make it happen."

Rather than a vision statement, this is more like a story as it creates powerful imagery. So why do I use this kind of emotional imagery?

The power of imagery ...

Whether you are a strong believer in the law of attraction, most people would agree that having positive thoughts has many benefits. This is no different to the workplace. The law of attraction claims that positive thinking can create life-changing results such as increased happiness, health and wealth.

*I emphasise to CEOs, you have to have a story
in the minds of the employees. It's hard to memorise
objectives, but it's easy to remember a story.*

Ben Horowitz

Many successful people claim to use positive thinking both consciously or unconsciously, attracting the success they want into their life by visualising their goals as already accomplished. This can be used for an organisation where a powerful image or visualisation of a desired outcome can harness the power of the people towards the future.

Visualisation is one of the primary tools used in sports psychology. The idea is that, "what happens out there (on the field) is a result of what happens in here (in each player's head)". In simple terms, this means our performance is often the result of what's happening inside our heads, or more specifically, the movies and soundtracks playing inside our heads.

Matt Neason from Sports Psychology Today says the most powerful effect of good visualisation is that it programs the subconscious brain. *"You want to think of the subconscious brain as a self-guiding missile. It identifies our co-ordinates and naturally moves us towards our target.*

"The problem with most people is that they program their subconscious mind with negative co-ordinates. They visualise images of failure, they replay mistakes, they think about negative scenarios that might happen, and picture the negative consequences that may arise. Unfortunately the subconscious mind (GPS) doesn't judge, it simply takes you to the programmed destination.

"The visualisation is important, but what's even more important is the feeling it creates inside of you. Create powerful emotions, and you'll create powerful performance states."

Business News Daily suggests imagining an article published about your company in five or ten years' time. What might it say? Ask yourself what the article might report as your organisation's biggest accomplishment. This might be worth putting in a vision!

By visualising success, you program your subconscious to move towards success

---

Job satisfaction, like happiness, is a state of mind...
Job satisfaction or employee satisfaction has been defined in many different ways. Some believe it's simply how content an individual is with his or her job. In other words, its whether or not they like the job or individual aspects or facets of the job, such as the nature of the work or the supervision.

In my view, happiness is a mental or emotional state of well-being, perhaps relating to quality of life, contentment, or even to joy.

Sonja Lyubomirsky concludes in her book The How of Happiness that 50% of a given human's happiness level is genetically determined (based on twin studies); 10% is affected by life circumstances and situation; and the remaining 40% of happiness is subject to self-control. Happiness is a matter of attitude, which can be influenced by leadership, people around us, our environment and ourselves.

In philosopher Ralph Waldo Emerson's words, "*with a positive attitude we experience pleasant and happy feelings. This brings brightness to the eyes, more energy, and an overall sense of joie de vivre that can be infectious. Our whole being broadcasts goodwill, contentment and success. Even our health is affected in a beneficial way. We walk tall, our voice is more powerful, and our body language shows the way we feel.*"

People don't notice whether it's winter or summer when they're happy.

Anton Chekhov

Employee comments:
"*My CEO practices what he preaches. All that you will read in this book is actually practiced (not theories) and the outcomes were excellent. I have personally grown ten-fold and to date it was the best place I have ever worked*"

Anand Sheth (Senior Manager)
Previous employee

In a nutshell...
Mission statements serve no purpose whatsoever and are of little benefit. They all look and sound like they have been written by a mission-statement generator. On the other hand, a vision statement is forward-looking and action-based. It gathers the momentum of the organisation. A simple powerful vision unifies the organisation's common purpose and direction. It is important to have a vision for the workplace culture.

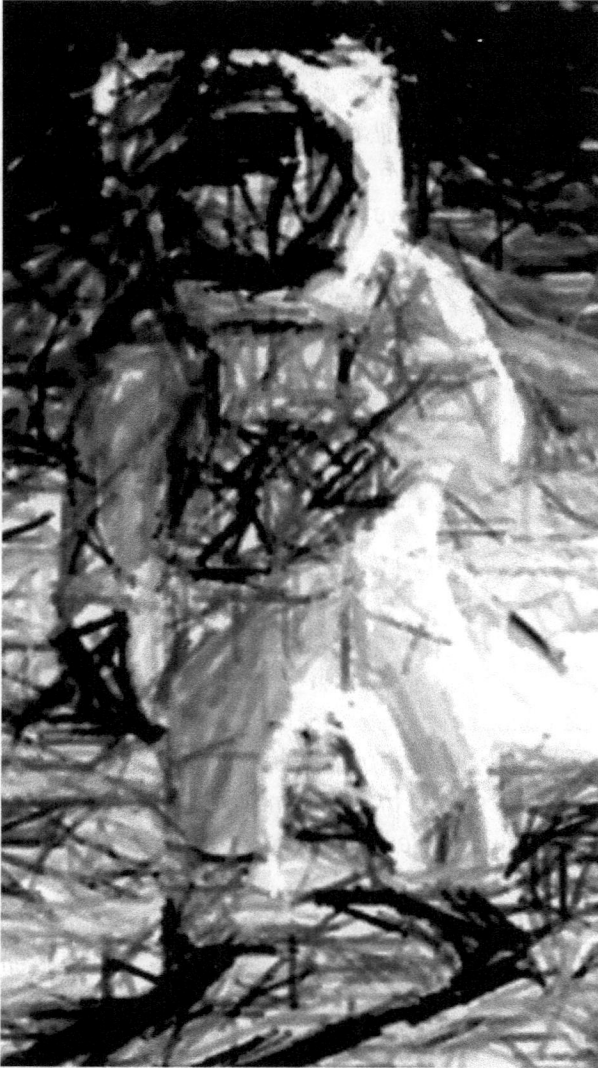

Motivation is the art of getting people to do what you want them to do because they want to do it.

Dwight D. Eisenhower

Chapter 10
Make decisions
without fear

Make decisions without fear

In this section I'm not going to try to breakdown the decision-making process but instead explain in my view how to go about providing the best environment for effective and dynamic decision-making.

You've probably worked for or are familiar with organisations where no one wants to make a final decision. At every opportunity more information is requested while the deadline for the decision looms closer. Instead of finalising a decision management just dithers or they may decide to go with one option but revisit it repeatedly. Management may also make poor (in hindsight) decisions that never translate into proper, effective action.

I'm sure you've seen many organisations struggle through these dysfunctional decision-making processes. It makes for a frustrating, painful and bureaucratic workplace. Wouldn't it be nice to work for an organisation where fast, dynamic, high-quality decision-making and execution is the norm?

Creating that kind of workplace...
This is my personal list of what is important in trying to create a workplace that encourages fearless decision-making:

1. Ensure you have a 'no blame' culture
2. There's no such thing as a right or wrong decision
3. Accept that you'll never have enough information
4. Know what you want
5. Making no decision at all is worse than making a wrong one
6. Identify who the actual decision-maker is
7. Use your innate intuition
8. How you manage once the decision is made is more important than the decision itself
9. Choose from a choice of one

'No blame' culture...

A 'no blame' culture is essential in creating a space for effective, dynamic decision-making. So what is a 'no blame' culture? Exactly that: no blame, no consequences when we get it wrong or when we make mistakes. As I wrote in Chapter 2, we've accidentally created a competitive blame culture through the performance appraisal system, the rewarding of individual performance rather than collective performance, and the need to be "looking good" amongst our peers. We've used job descriptions as a tool to allocate blame when things go wrong.

Without open, honest and transparent communication, people focus on advancing their own agenda and the fear of decision-making grows when a mistake is made. In this sort of environment, why would you ever want to, or submit to being forced to make a decision? Feelings of vulnerability and guilt are not aspects of a workplace culture that would inspire effective, high-performing teamwork.

No right or wrong decisions...

Organisations can be paranoid about making the right decision and avoiding the wrong one. I believe there's no such thing as a right or wrong decision. Any decision is made at a point in time with appropriate facts, information, arguments, emotion and intuition.

It's only in hindsight or further in time that you see the consequences of that decision. It's only with a little bit of extra information (hindsight) that you can judge the quality of that decision. Unless you have access to a crystal ball that can see into the future, the result of any decision can only be assessed through the progression of time and hindsight.

For example, the decision to marry someone is based on many factors that are presented to you at the time. Essentially you weren't 100% sure (unless you had that crystal ball) at the time whether it was a good or bad decision. After a while, if you're happily married, you look back and think it was the best decision you made. But if you're unhappily married, divorced or separated, then you'd probably look back and think it was one of your worst decisions. The progression of time and consequences allowed you to evaluate that prior decision. With the same facts, information, arguments, emotion and intuition, you'd make exactly the same decision. So stop worrying about making a wrong one.

**There's no such thing as a wrong decision,
just make a decision**

You'll never have enough information...
Organisations that continually stall decision-making to allow time to collect more and more facts and information are frustrating workplaces.

You've heard the term "paralysis by analysis": it means over-analysing (or over-thinking) a situation so that a decision is never made and an action never initiated. The decision is treated as over-complicated, accompanied by too many detailed options, and in the end a choice is never made. Often organisations seek the optimal or "perfect" solution upfront and fear making any decision, which leads to erroneous results (like how you chose your spouse).

It's always ideal to have every fact and information at your disposal when making decisions. But life's not like that. What will my spouse be like in five years' time, or when we have children, when she reaches menopause, or he hits a mid-life crisis?

It is difficult to collect, collate and analyse all the supporting information that comes with making a decision. Often we have to make do with what we have, use intuition, and go ahead and decide.

Gayle Abbott, president of human resources consulting firm Strategic Alignment Partners, said that when it comes down to it, the answer may not always be clear, even when using a rational decision-making process.

"Sometimes you've got to say, 'I've now gathered all of this information and it is time to act," Abbott said. *"The most successful people don't have to have all the information. They are willing to take risks. A big part of it is knowing when to be decisive."*

A director friend of mine tells me that you have to recognise what you don't know and plan to manage the unknowns. Risk management is highly important in the decision-making process. This is a very important area of running an organisation. Planning ahead or being "two steps ahead" with contingency plans in place is encouraged in our organisations in order to manage the potential risks of decisions. We say that if we were playing a game of chess, for example, what would our move be two or three turns from now?

Know what you want...
Often the management within an organisation has not spent the time identifying what they want before embarking on the decision-making process. They often rely on gathering all the information and generating choices to help them find what it is they actually want.

My view is that if you know the main criteria that you can't compromise on, and you acknowledge the desired outcomes, decision-making would be relatively easy. There will always be some compromise in decisions but they can be made quickly and efficiently.

Above all, Abbott said, keep your eyes on the prize. "Be clear on the ultimate objective," she said. "When faced with choices or options, you need to choose the one that will most quickly achieve it. Know your strengths and weaknesses to stay out of trouble."

No decision is worse than a poor decision...

In our organisations people are encouraged to make decisions quickly and effectively. Our philosophy is that there are no wrong decisions and delaying decisions (unless you are waiting for some pre-determined, specific data) isn't encouraged. People are often very attached to the status quo. Decisions tend to involve the prospect of change, which many people find difficult. Supported by a non-blame culture, people are encouraged to be dynamic, nimble and flexible.

As president Theodore Roosevelt said, *"In any moment of decision, the best you can do is the right thing, the next best thing is the wrong thing, and the worst thing you can do is nothing."*

Fundamentally, there is an opportunity lost in not making a decision: any decision is better than none.

Identifying who the decision-maker is...

Part of the problem is recognising the decision-maker within an organisation. In larger companies, it's often very hard to pin-point the decision-making procedure and difficult to then determine the final decision-maker. Making decisions by committee is challenging as everyone has their own views and values. While it's important to know what these views are and why and how they're important, in the end, one person should be responsible for making the final decision.

**the process is much simpler if everyone knows
who will make the ultimate decision**

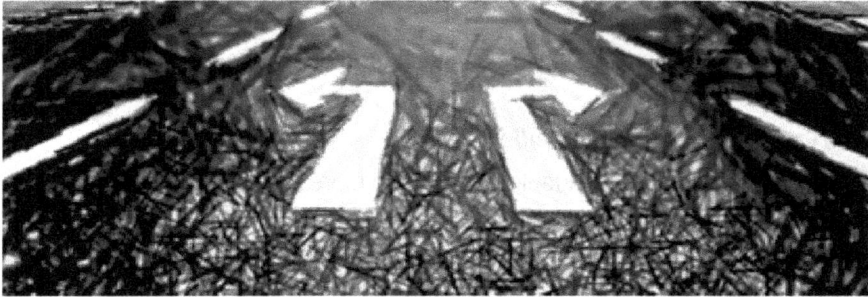

In my business of bringing strategic investors to the company, my job mainly consists of presenting or pitching to an audience. While I'm happy to make introductory presentations, I always insist on seeing the main decision-maker as soon as I can. Otherwise, the whole investment proposal gets stuck within middle management and no one is game enough to push it up the decision-making tree without loads of accompanying information and data.

When I do get to the decision-maker, let's say the chairman of the company, he or she will either like it or not. Often they use their experience, intuition, and the feeling (confidence and passion) they get from the presenter. If the feeling is positive, the investment moves rapidly through due diligence and the process is relatively quick. Without the actual decision-maker's involvement early on, the investment presentation is almost a waste of time.

Professors Melissa Cardon (Pace University), Cheryl Mitteness (Northeastern University) and Richard Sudek (Chapman University) performed a remarkable experiment and published the results in the September 2012 issue of the Journal of Business Venturing. They set out to understand the role that passion plays in investor decision-making.

The investment pitch is one of the most critical presentations in business and the researchers concluded that 'perceived passion' does make a difference when investors evaluate the funding potential of new ventures. Perceived passion involves enthusiasm, excitement and is distinct from how prepared or committed an entrepreneur may be to their venture. This is no different to the leader's passion about the vision of their organisation.

Use your intuition and gut feeling...

Innate intuition or one's 'gut feeling' is gaining more and more recognition as an essential decision-making tool. You've probably heard of experienced decision-makers who are able to directly recognise the best option or the best course of action in many tricky situations. The solution usually just comes to them from somewhere in their subconscious mind. Intuition is described as a phenomenon of the mind's ability to acquire knowledge without inference or the use of reason.

glimpses of greater knowledge through processes, which remain mostly unknown to the thinker

In Eastern philosophy, intuition is mostly intertwined with religion and spirituality with many references to Hinduism, Buddhism and Islam philosophy. References of intuition can be traced back to Plato where he defined intuition as a fundamental capacity of human reason to comprehend the true nature of reality.

Intuition, as a 'gut feeling' based on experience, has been found to be useful for business leaders making judgements about people, culture and strategy. Gayle Abbott, president of Strategic Alignment Partners who we've already met in this chapter, is a supporter of listening to your intuition. *"The best leaders do this, and then gather all the facts and data to either support or reject that gut feeling,"* Abbott said. *"Intuition is a perfectly acceptable means of making a decision, although it is generally more appropriate when the decision is of a simple nature or needs to be made quickly."*

Instinct evolved for a reason – it works really well. To our Stone Age ancestors having the ability to make a snap decision could've made the difference between being eaten by a sabre-toothed tiger and enjoying one for dinner. Innate intuition or gut feeling enabled humankind to survive over the millennia. It protected us from harm and predators as we "sensed" danger lurking close by. We made life or death decisions based on instinct. It became a highly developed tool for decision-making and survival.

Today, we couldn't justify a decision in any organisation without masses of supporting data, information and justification. We certainly couldn't say that "it felt like it was the right thing to do".

An important thing to always keep in mind is that even when you rely on intuition it's still very important to do your homework. The intuition will help you navigate faster through much of the unstructured data and you will work around certain gaps and conflicts in the available information. Yet, even intuition can be distorted if too many of your facts are wrong or missing.

We're discouraged to use intuition...

While most of us might have relied upon intuition when we were younger, we might have been discouraged from using this powerful tool during childhood. When we were very young and were allowed to choose a toy our parents might have asked why we picked that particular one. The child's answer, "I just did." Parents would press for more information, "you must have a good reason for why you chose it. Was it the colour? Was it the softness or smell? Was it the shape?" Mum and dad wouldn't let it go without a logical reason.

So we learnt quickly as young children that we had to have a logical reason to justify our decisions. We were trained to come up with a rational explanation to support the choices we made, suppressing that most powerful tool, an innate intuition or gut feeling.

> *Sometimes you make the right decision,*
> *sometimes you make the decision right.*
>
> Phil McGraw

Chaotic, unpredictable and unexpected things happen...

Most people want to know how things will pan out before they make a decision. This is usually counterproductive. Based on my early premise that there are no right or wrong decisions, I'd say that in life, a decision made opens up the energy flow, which then leads to certain desired or undesired outcomes. The world is chaotic, unpredictable and unexpected things happen.

Based on this, new solutions can be proposed, alternate pathways open up, new decisions can be made and so life goes on. Life's journey has many forked roads and decisions are made along the way. Not making a decision at the first fork stops the energy flow that's part of life. If you made a commitment to something in the past that's no longer useful for you, you've allowed yourself to give up that commitment.

As Gayle Abbott says, *"when you see a successful person, you do not see what happened behind the scenes. All of them have made mistakes on their way up, but they move on. They have struggled through failures – bad decisions – before finding a solution."*

---

what you do after the decision
is more important than the decision itself

Making a choice of one...

My daughter Emma lives in Sydney where she works as a dentist. I was visiting her and we were talking about the khaki-coloured coat she was wearing. It didn't look very warm and it wasn't all that attractive so I offered to buy her a new winter coat; and being a graduate dentist with low funds in her bank account, she accepted.

So we went shopping. We proceeded to the department store where we ascended the escalators at Myer. Arriving on the first floor, I saw a rack of David Lawrence coats and immediately found a dark blue one with a nice cut and trendy looking panels.

I showed it to Emma and she liked it straight away. I said *"let's get it,"* but Emma started to back off. *"You know it takes me at least two hours of shopping to buy a coat so let's look around some more,"* she suggested.

In this case, Emma was presented with a *"choice of one"* and most people have difficulty making a choice from one option. We often need reference points to make us feel that our decision is correct.

"Emma, you clearly like the coat, the colour is perfect and it looks great on you" (in other words, it meets all her upfront criteria). She agreed with me. *"Now you want to look around some more on the slim chance you'll find another coat that you like as much or find others not as good so it reinforces your initial choice? Are we going to waste two hours of frustrated shopping just so we can arrive back at this purchase?"* We bought the coat and went to lunch.

Employee comments:

"Blame from colleagues or supervisors has always brought nervous emotion in my previous career and prevented me from taking more responsibility. The "no blame" culture created here has brought a relaxed atmosphere, unites the team as one and encourages everyone to make more of an effort to achieve company targets. It has been a joy working for this company".

Martin Ma (Sales Manager)
Previous employee

In a nutshell...

A 'no blame' culture is essential in the workplace as it allows people to make decisions without fear. The underlying philosophy is that there is no such thing as a right or wrong decision. The organisation recognises that not all the information is needed at the time but any decision is more important than no decision. Innate intuition is encouraged.

Risk management is highly important in the decision-making process. Planning ahead or being "two steps ahead" and having contingency plans in place are encouraged in our organisations in order to manage the potential risks of decisions.

This hopefully nurtures an organisation where fast, dynamic, high-quality, fearless decision-making and execution are the norm.

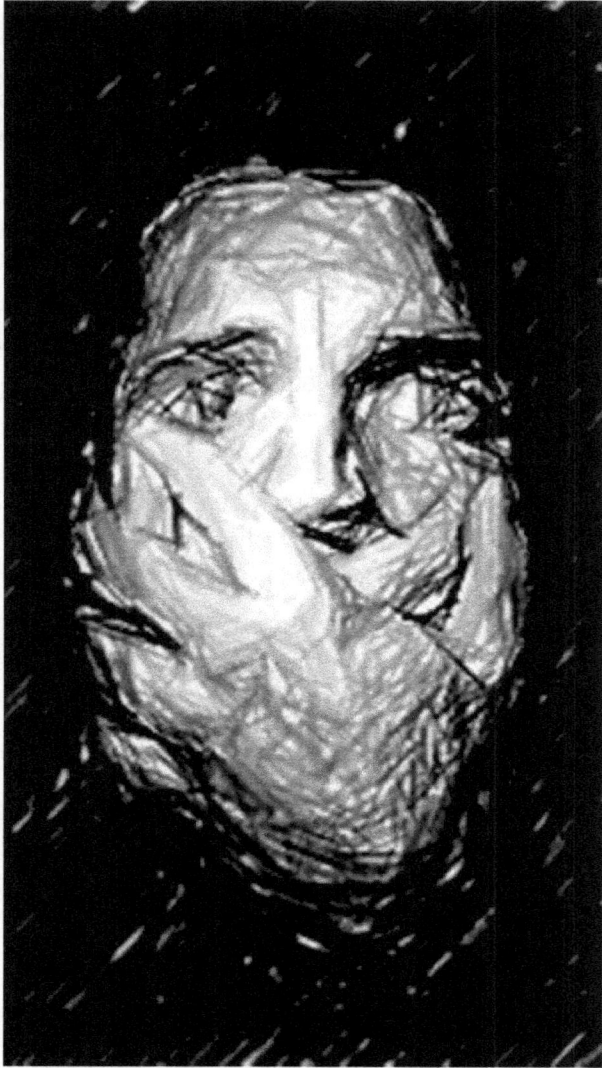

Informed decision-making comes from a long tradition of guessing and then blaming others for inadequate results.
Scott Adams

Chapter 11
Throw out the CV when recruiting

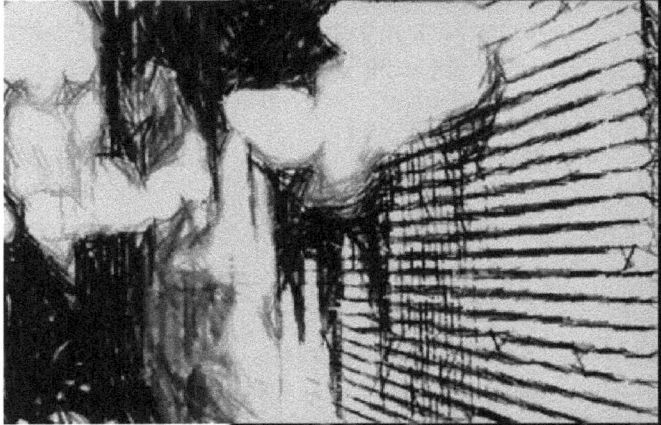

Throw out the CV when recruiting

Recruitment is another significant area of modern day management which attracts a lot of focus and concern. I don't know how many times I've heard the phrase "we'll find you the best person for the job." Recruitment firms have always perpetuated this notion where, with their processes, database, networks and various tools such as psychology testing they'll produce the "best person for the job." They'll often back up their placement work with a guarantee period so if the candidate does not work out, free recruitment will be provided to find a replacement.

The "best person for the job" idea is similar to the idea of organisations recruiting the "top performers" to join their company. There's no such thing as the best or the top person for a role within a company; this is a flawed and dangerous idea.

Find someone that fits in the best…

The recruitment policy within our organisations is not to find the "best person for the job". While finding someone who can do the job is a requirement, most importantly, we find someone who fits into the workplace culture the best. We look for a suitable person for the job who fits in, who can contribute to the workplace harmony and the productivity of our team environment. If they're a team player, they'll help others achieve, they'll co-operate, collaborate, be inclusive and enhance the overall team dynamics. That's the best fit we look for.

You're trying to pick people that fit into the culture of a company.
Tim Cook, CEO of Apple Inc.

After all, upsetting the dynamics, teamwork and workplace culture will have dire consequences. It's taken many years of hard work to mould the organisation into a high-performing group with team-based principles. Hiring a rogue, self-centred candidate will not only be detrimental but will adversely affect the morale of the group leading to potential set-backs in productivity, creativity and decision-making.

Let's accept that sometimes you're going to get it wrong…

We're so scared of getting it wrong in recruiting that we're prepared to pay large recruitment fees and fund all sorts of testing such as IQ, EQ, and psychological appraisals as well as many rounds of interviews and reference checking.

Despite all the pre-screening we still get "wrong fits". I'm sure in your experience you've seen the complicated recruitment processes that still end up with a complete "a-hole" who does not fit into the team.

Don't you think that people (like ourselves when we apply for jobs) have learnt to say the right things and include all the right details in their CV's? Ticking the right boxes in psychological tests and displaying the right behaviour in the interview process? Of course, we all have and recruiters have trained us to do all those things. This complex recruitment process has made us believe it is the right and only way to hire people.

In the previous chapter I discussed making decisions without fear; this theory also applies to the recruitment process. There's no such thing as a right or wrong decision, so if you're a manager, make a selection and trust your innate intuition. Don't waste time by revisiting your options and gathering more information. Accept that, say one in ten times, it may not work out and the candidate may not fit in with the team as you expected. Life isn't perfect. Embrace that this is going to happen sometimes and don't be fearful of it. Be prepared to deal with the situation when it happens.

**what is more important than the decision itself
is what you do after the decision is made**

Throw the CV away...

Sure, the CV is an ideal tool to determine a candidate's background, experience, skills and eventually their qualifications to do the job. Use the CV to get to your interview shortlist but after that throw it away. During the interview process, instead of addressing the details written on their CV, managers should be focusing on whether the candidate has similar values and aspirations as the organisation and team they're about to join. You are searching for someone who has passion, who will fit in and enhance your workplace culture. A friend of mine in small business management believes this crucial explaining, *"I use the interviews to ask the non-technical questions to get my gut feel for the person and their fit for the company"*.

While Virgin Group founder Richard Branson credits the importance of a resume, he prefers to discover a candidate's passions and all the compelling details about a candidate's life that aren't necessarily appropriate for inclusion in a corporate resume.

In a recent 2015 Ted Talk, Regina Hartley spoke about her views of why the best candidate may not have the best resume. She spoke about "strapper" vs "silver spoon" candidates. Silver spoon candidates had impeccable CVs, clearly had advantages and were destined for success. On the other hand, strapper candidates had to fight against tremendous odds and suffered early hardships to get to the same point. She called this "post-traumatic growth".

"Companies that are committed to diversity and inclusive practices tend to support strappers and outperform their peers. Choose the underestimated contender whose secret weapon is passion and purpose," she said.

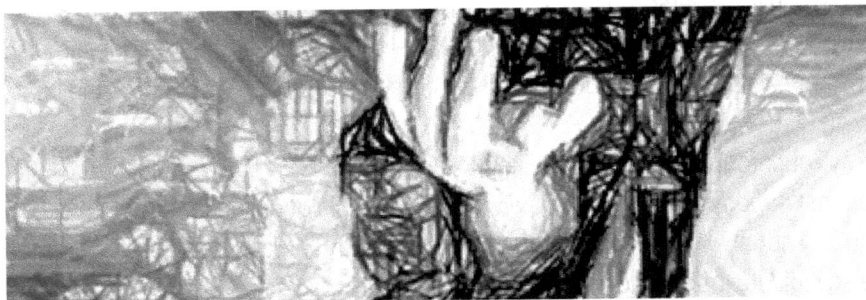

The question is how do we find someone that fits in well? By throwing away the CV we can focus and rely solely on other clues like our innate intuition or gut feeling as part of the selection process. This intuition or "gut feeling" is an individual's "common sense" perception based on emotional feelings and not on any logic or facts.

I spoke to a professional recruitment friend of mine the other day who admitted to recruiting people based on intuition. She said she has the innate ability to pick candidates that fit the clients' organisation and culture. I guess most professional recruiters would say the same to their clients. In order to recruit these recruiters have to firstly understand the company and team culture, which is hard to do when they're not immersed in it.

What to ask?

In recruitment today we're paranoid about what can and can't be asked at a job interview. According to discrimination law, questions should be job-related and not used to find out personal information. In general, employers should avoid questions about race, gender, religion, marital status, age, disabilities, ethnic background, country of origin, sexual preferences, age or interests. But the truth is that we are more interested in details that aren't given on the CV. We want to ascertain if the person will be a good fit with the teamwork culture that is present. Still, we go through this merry dance of asking carefully structured questions in the hope that we find out more about the person than what was stated in their CV.

PayPal cofounder Peter Thiel likes to ask, *"Tell me something that's true, that almost nobody agrees with you on."* Thiel asks this question in order to pinpoint an individual who isn't afraid to speak their mind. The candidate's answer may also indicate the courage to speak up at difficult times.

"What makes you happy about a great working day?" This is a paraphrase of a question that Lew Cirne, founder of US software analysis company New Relic often asks. The question is a clever conversational incentive and interview tactic that gets a candidate to discuss the sources of their enjoyment at work.

I often like to hold a candidate interview in a more relaxed setting, like lunch or coffee, where an informal chat is likely to transpire and we get to know each other. I like to come to understand the candidate's background, experience and philosophies. For the benefit of both parties, we need to really get to know each other to ensure that there's going to be a good fit. It doesn't serve the new candidate's interest if they were sold a job opportunity in a workplace culture that was not a reality. How many times have you started a job and then asked yourself *"what am I getting myself into here?"*

In most job interviews, people say they are looking for people skills and emotional intelligence. That's reasonable, but the question is, how do you define what that looks like?

Susan Cain

Talk about the culture...

I generally spend most of the interview process describing to the candidate the kind of workplace culture we have, which helps to get the candidate's guard down. I try to describe the actual behaviours within the organisation rather than desired values. For example, I tell the candidate that we don't have performance appraisals and then provide the reasons behind that philosophy. "We don't reward individual performance but team outcomes, we ban individual KPIs, and we work hard at always using open, honest, transparent communication. Our job description is simple: do "whatever it takes" to help others to achieve the team outcomes." As we talk, I generally get a reaction of some sort. Often the passion in the candidate's eyes and response tells me that they will be a good fit. The candidate might say, "I've always believed that performance appraisals were a complete waste of time".

In a nutshell...

The recruitment policy for an organisation should not be to find the "best person for the job", rather, find someone who firstly can do the job, but most importantly, fits into the workplace culture the best. Someone who contributes to the workplace harmony and the productivity of the team environment. By throwing away the CV at the interview stage we can focus and rely solely on other clues like our innate intuition or gut feeling as part of the recruitment selection process.

Chapter 12
Having to
dismiss employees

Having to dismiss employees

How to dismiss employees? Exactly the same way you would prefer to be dismissed yourself.

Nick's story...

Let me tell you the story about Nick, a friend of mine. Nick worked for a large Swiss-owned international engineering firm for about eight years as a contract manager. He was a good performer and progressed to be a manager of his small section that deal with the design and contract sales of large process equipment.

During 2014, the mining industry in Western Australia was in severe recession and many companies were making staff redundant. Nick's company had already made several rounds of cut-backs and redundancies and everyone was anticipating further downsizing. One day, out of the blue, Nick was asked for a meeting with the HR department, which he attended without his manager present.

The HR manager told him that his position was being made redundant. Nick was shocked by the announcement. When people around you are being let go, you often think you'll be able to hang on somehow. His termination and support package was explained to him. He was asked to clear his desk, not to tell anyone in his section and leave the workplace. Nick left without saying goodbye as instructed and was never seen again in the organisation.

After around eight years of loyal service, is this is how we should treat an employee when there's a termination?

The day before the company decided on this course, Nick was a valuable, trusted employee who was appreciated for his long and loyal service. The minute he was made redundant he no longer had value, he was distrusted and he became a liability for the firm and other employees. As you can expect, Nick was devastated. He became depressed and took a long time to recover from the ordeal. He later discovered that his manager only found out he had gone a month later. I'm sure a similar story is common in your personal experience and in the organisations that you've worked for. Often companies don't care about people's mental state and health once they are no longer it's employees.

So how did Nick's colleagues react to his redundancy when they rocked up to work the next day? They'd have asked, "Where's Nick?" and seeing his empty desk, people might have just assumed that the aliens had taken him!

The rest of the organisation starts to realise that, like Nick, their real value to the business is zilch and that the stated values and integrity on the wall plaque are just "words on the wall". Employees lose respect for their organisation when incidents like Nick's occur and are so badly handled.

Now think about what would have happened if Nick actually resigned on his own accord, due to say another job opportunity. He would work his notice period out, and being professional, he'd complete any work that was outstanding and pass on unfinished work to other colleagues. Staff would have organised a going-away function where the company would thank Nick for his valuable service and maybe present him with an appreciation gift.

Nick would have had the chance to say goodbye to those people he worked with for the last eight years and it would have been a fitting end to that part of his career.

That's what most people who have given many years of loyal and dedicated service would expect from an organisation. That would be indicative of the basic common courtesy and decency with which you would treat a fellow human being. Everyone can see the difference in the above two scenarios. Yet why, as organisations, do we treat people so badly when we make them redundant? I've heard all the reasons from management, HR and legal about managing the risk, the possibility of litigation or de-stabilising the organisation, the risk of sabotage or stealing and all the other excuses for getting people off-site as quickly possible.

Frankly, I don't buy it. We have to stand up for the values of our workplace culture through our behaviour right to the very end. And often there is a risk associated with it, but that becomes the test of your conviction.

If you treat people with respect and trust, they'll understand the situation and behave professionally like they always have. In the end they're still relying on final termination payments so there's always an incentive to behave professionally. People often understand why jobs need to be lost due to economic situations but what people get upset about is "how it's done".

If you hire, you fire...

In workplaces today I am seeing the unpleasant task of firing being passed from supervisor or manager to the HR department. Particularly in large organisations, termination or redundancy meetings are more commonly being conducted by the HR people without interaction from line supervisors or managers.

As you can see from Nick's story, at no point was line management involved in the termination process. If you go back to the philosophy of this book, back to the basics of management, let supervisors and managers manage their people. If you hire, you fire. As a supervisor or manager you must have the courage and courtesy to be able to manage your people in good times and in bad times.

Tell them when they have a pay rise or promotion, but also tell them directly when they are not performing or when they have been made redundant. There are many studies that show the trust level is the highest between an employee and his/her direct supervisor. The best way to deal with an event like a redundancy is between the supervisor and employee with support from HR. This is a common courtesy that we should extend to our employees, instead of HR handling all terminations, which is becoming a common trend for companies in Australia.

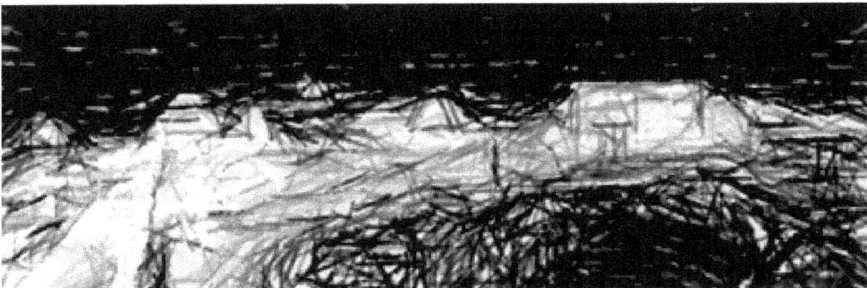

Exactly the same way you would prefer to be dismissed...

Due to the economic situation at the time, as well as commodity prices and exchange rates, we had to put a mine in care and maintenance and make a workforce of around 100 redundant. After weeks of planning, we flew to the mine site to address the workforce. We briefed levels of management (not generally done by other companies) earlier so that they could get over the shock to then be able to support the staff and explain the support packages.

Instead of locking the gates and sending everyone home, we explained the situation and said that we wanted everyone to work their notice period out. We provided good redundancy packages. During this time, we wanted everyone to place the plant into care and maintenance in a professional manner.

Whilst these employees continued to come to work every day, we had consulting companies help with their CVs. We organised other mining companies looking for staff to come in and interview potential candidates. We took over their housing rental leases so that if they secured a job straight away, they could leave without being tied down with their leases. We also provided a relocation allowance so that they could move to their new jobs immediately as most would not have savings to cover the costs.

The workforce conducted themselves in a professional manner and returned the trust and integrity that we placed with them. At the end of the notice period, we had a farewell function for all the employees and their families and provided a gift of appreciation for their loyal service. In the end, we found jobs for nearly half the workforce before they left our care.

I don't know how many people and their families thanked us dearly for the way we had treated them. They all said that they would come back and work for us in a heartbeat. I guess things can be done differently.

Employee comments:

"Executive management conducted the mine closure with the utmost integrity, fairness and compassion toward its employees, contractors and families. During my 40 years within the industry I am not aware of, nor have experienced any other business that had considered it's employees' and their families' wellbeing at times of stress.

The support for employees/families during redundancy was invaluable.

Although employees were initially shocked due to not knowing the way forward, they were also disappointed of the closure as they had a sense of belonging and were proud of their achievements.

Employees did not feel discarded and abandoned. The most stressful elements of redundancy were offset and they were supported until they were able to secure other employment, move home and families.

Each employee I had spoken with had a great appreciation to the company for its support; they said they'd wish to be re-employed if the mine was to restart."

Roger Pover (Manager)
Previous employee

In a nutshell...

Having to dismiss employees is difficult for both the employee as well as the organisation. The way we dismiss employees should be exactly the same way that you would prefer to be dismissed yourself; hopefully with some respect and dignity and the acknowledgment of the valuable loyalty and service you've provided.

Chapter 13
Two steps ahead

Two steps ahead

Planning ahead or being "two steps ahead" while reinforcing positive thinking as a standard principle of behaviour creates proactive, healthy, energetic and efficient organisations. The challenge for managers is allowing employees the freedom to utilise these principles to do their job and achieve the overall targets without micromanagement.

Micromanaging...

Micromanaging is very common in today's workplace and you can spot a micromanager from a mile away. They are so controlling about the tasks assigned to their employees that it totally discourages employees from taking responsibility for their work. Instead of focusing on the tiny details, we encourage our managers to focus on the agreed results, outcomes and 'big picture' objectives. We need to allow our employees the latitude to decide how they will achieve them. Our employees are given the freedom to get on with their tasks in the way they see fit.

The challenge for managers is how to behave it in order for it to translate into the workplace culture. The balance between being aware of what is going on and giving freedom to employees to make things happen is very difficult to achieve. In the end the buck stops with the leader and unfortunately some fall into the trap of extreme control to the point of micromanagement. In my experience micromanagement is the symptom of the workplace culture. Micromanagement is often signified by an authoritative management culture, which creates blame, low morale and internal office politics. American billionaire investor Ray Dalio describes micromanaging as telling the people who work for you exactly what tasks to do and/or doing their tasks for them. Not micromanaging is having them do their jobs without your oversight and involvement.

Google, in an effort to prevent micromanagement within their corporation of over 37,000 staff, restructured their engineering management resulting in the department's managers having as many as 30 staff reporting direct. *"There is only so much you can meddle when you have 30 people on your team, so you have to focus on creating the best environment for engineers to make things happen,"* Google engineer Eric Flatt says.

Tim Berry from Business Insider described micromanagement as a "real drag". *"It's hard to do and annoying as hell. Hire smart people who share your business values, give them ownership of what they do, and trust them. The real test is when they get bad results or do things differently than you would have."*

Think positively...

In our organisations, we encourage our people to think challenges not problems. Daily reinforcement of basic positive thinking and acting in a positive manner within the workplace creates a healthier, happier and more effective working environment. Whether you are a strong believer in the law of attraction, most people would agree that an organisation with positive thoughts and actions has many benefits. Ultimately, working in a negatively-charged workplace is very unpleasant.

I am sure you have experienced staff constantly whinging or complaining of their unhappiness at work. These are vitality and energy-zapping environments.

Acting positively affects the culture and in turn affects overall morale. It doesn't mean that we don't address negative issues at all. Unexpected situations or poor results are dealt with from a strictly optimistic perspective. Using this outlook allows the company to look at itself honestly and stay alert to possible threats.

Success or failure in business is caused more by the mental attitude even than by mental capacities.

Walter Scott

In 1938 journalist Napoleon Hill studied 500 wealthy men over 20 years and boiled down their success to positive thinking and emotions. *"Positive and negative emotions cannot occupy the mind at the same time. One or the other must dominate. It is your responsibility to make sure that positive emotions constitute the dominating influence of your mind. If you want to be successful it is critical that the positive emotions dominate any negative ones that arise."* Other research in this field shows that positive, happier people are more likely to perform better at their jobs.

Undertake the right things...

Doing everything the right way becomes an obsession for bureaucratic organisations: there must be one right, formal and documented way of doing things. Countless forms need to be filled out and boxes ticked. These companies manage their strict procedures through complex systems that require hours and hours of resources to manage and implement. No one ever questions the benefits but instead more and more systems are implemented with more and more forms in the hope of improving company performance. Sometimes there is a form required to create another form and one to remove a form from circulation! In our organisations we focus on **doing the right things** rather than doing things right. We continue to simplify the business and cut out the office politics. A suitable catch phrase that (by chance) came up during one of our weekly meetings was Nike's slogan – JUST DO IT! – and it stuck around, becoming one of our philosophies.

Almost all quality improvement comes via simplification of design, manufacturing... layout, processes, and procedures.

Tom Peters

Two steps ahead...

Some organisations are like fire-fighters: they are great at solving emergency problems as they arise. They launch into crisis meetings, adrenalin pumping through the veins of participants, reactions are heightened, and the problems are solved and actioned quickly. They return to their station to wait for another emergency crisis to fix. The reactionary rush of the adrenalin becomes a real addiction for these organisations.

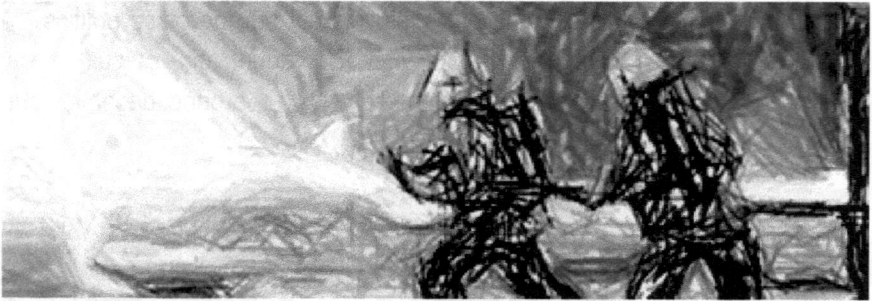

In our organisations we encourage our people to plan ahead or to be "two steps ahead", while negating this kind of emergency crisis management. We encourage people to foresee and anticipate problems and issues before they occur. Imagine how calm and collected an organisation would be if it had access to a magic crystal ball and could see all the problems that were coming up? With this insight into the future, we could be well prepared for any crisis or issue likely to arise. That 'crystal ball' mentality is what we try to develop in our organisations where we are constantly trying to be two steps ahead.

To develop the intuition and forward planning approach (unfortunately we don't have a crystal ball) we play a game of being two steps ahead of the boss. *"What will my boss most likely ask me for in the near future?"* The answer cannot refer to something that is a standard business matter such as a regular report or budget.

So for example, due to recent news on falling exchange rates, a team leader anticipates the need for a financial impact analysis. *"My boss hasn't asked me yet but I expect they will within the month."* Now that the team leader has forecast a possible requirement, the idea is to go ahead and commence the work and file it away in preparation for that request down the track. If it comes up at a meeting later and the boss enquires, *"I am concerned about the recent changes in the exchange rates and I think we should get someone to analyse the impact on our business"*, the leader replies, *"we have already conducted the analysis and my recommendation is..."*!

The game or practice of being two steps ahead (of your boss) and turning these opportunities into plans and actions before they come up creates a very proactive workplace culture. Reinforcing this practice creates a calmer, controlled and relaxed management culture when dealing with problems. We say that if we were playing a game of chess, what would our move be two or three turns from now. We don't react; we act and lead with a sense of urgency. We get involved and make a difference.

The power of positive affirmation...

In one of my operations we had a situation where we were hoping to reach a production record in three months' time. It would be a very significant milestone, the highest output achieved in the history of the plant. Thinking two steps ahead of my boss, I thought that if we achieved the record target, he would ask me for a congratulatory letter to the employees and some milestone celebration. I went ahead and prepared everything like it already happened. The congratulatory letter was drafted and filed away. When the record was eventually broken, my boss requested the letter that I anticipated and I produced it according to the plan (two steps ahead).

Once you make a decision,
the universe conspires to make it happen.

Ralph Waldo Emerson

Aiming to be 'two steps ahead' is also important in maintaining positive energy and tapping into the power of self-fulfilling prophesy. The draft record production letter creates the 'intention' energy that is a form of visualisation programming the subconscious mind. In Chapter 9, I discuss the power of visualisation used in sports performance. This works exactly the same way: positive visualisation programs the subconscious brain and, like a self-guiding missile, naturally moves us towards our target.

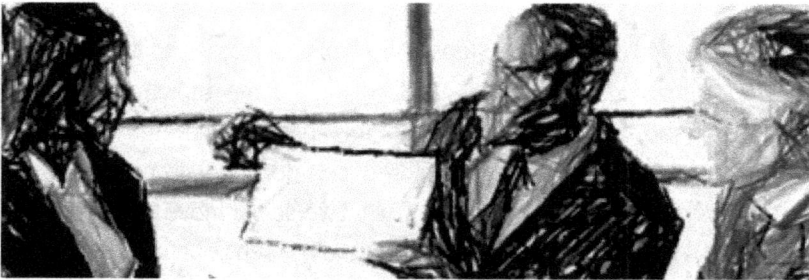

In Napoleon Hill's study of 500 wealthy men, this visualising success theory planted in the subconscious mind of the men was a key factor of their success. If you can imagine it, you can create it, says Hill.

"Man's only limitation, within reason, lies in his development and use of his imagination. Once you've visualised your success, you need to take action and go after exactly what you want. You must act with persistence and enthusiasm".

When significant events occur, as a public company, we are required to lodge company announcements to the stock exchange. As part of ways to create positive intentions and visualisations, we would often draft an announcement on something that hadn't occurred yet but we wished for that outcome, and then file the draft away. These powerful positive affirmations, in the form of draft announcements, created the intentional energy for success. This is no different to an athlete's positive visualisation used in his or her sport.

*The idea of investing in the positivity of employees is often
low down on companies priority lists.*

Shawn Achor

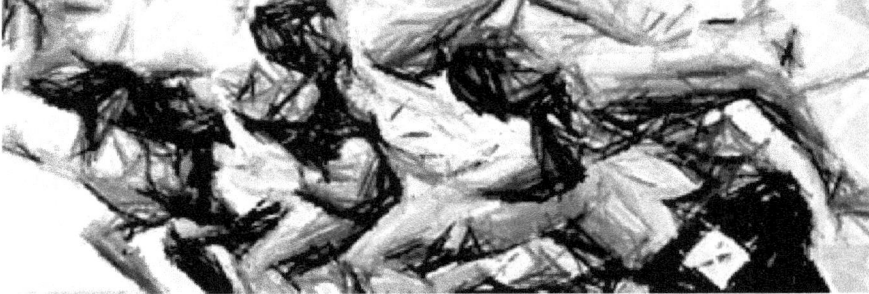

I recall a time when I was courting a major Chinese investor and I wasn't sure if a deal was on the cards. I wrote an announcement as though we achieved success with the investor and filed it away. The deal eventually dissipated and we went our merry ways. About 18 months later, the same Chinese party was re-introduced to us again, which this time resulted in a large injection of capital for the company.

I had to write up an announcement and guess what, I picked the original announcement I had drafted 18 months prior. A date change and some minor number updates were required before it was ready to go. This is a very powerful tool that organisations can use to create positive, self-fulfilling visualisations. It works most of the time.

In a nutshell...

Basic positive thinking and acting in a positive manner within the workplace will create a healthier, happier and more effective working environment. The behaviour of acting in a positive manner (behaviour) affects the culture and overall morale. Organisations must strive to focus on doing the right things rather than doing things right and in the process, simplify the business and cut out the office politics.

The culture of thinking and being 'two steps ahead' by taking those actions ahead of time creates a very proactive workplace culture. The benefit is a calmer, controlled and relaxed management culture when dealing with problems. Visualisation of successes is a powerful way for organisations to program the subconscious mind, set the intentional energy, the positive energy and tap into the power of self-fulfilling prophesy to achieve the organisation's goals.

Chapter 14
Key to driving cultural change

Key to driving cultural change

In this book I address the idea of establishing a workplace culture from inception. But what about driving cultural change in established organisations?

Cultural change...

I guess in my job as a manager of operations or as a head of companies, I've had many challenges instigating cultural change within an established organisation or operation. It's probably one of the hardest things to do as a manager. If you understand that culture is a collective set of behaviours within an organisation, how do you change all those well-established and entrenched behaviours? I guess it can be done but it requires a lot of passion, persistence and patience.

In one of these change appointments, I was appointed general manager of a mining and processing operation. The operation had a workforce of nearly 800 people including contractors spread across two sites. My role was to improve the efficiency and the profitability of the business. The staff had suffered a change of ownership and morale was very low. To achieve any sort of business turnaround, I needed to capture the hearts and minds of the entire workforce.

If I had to sum up the two main things I targeted to effect this (and every) turnaround they'd be:
1. Housekeeping
2. Communication

It sounds deceptively simple, yet it works and gets the biggest bang for your buck on the cultural change front.

Housekeeping...

Usually the housekeeping of an operation with cultural issues is poor. As an experienced manager, you learn that general housekeeping and neatness are the pulse of morale, efficiency and health of the organisation. When people and management feel good about the culture of the workplace, they care for the workplace and vice versa.

In my case, the first thing that we got underway was a massive clean-up of the whole site. In some cases, this could take months and months of extensive work as a site is usually very deteriorated and poorly looked after. Getting everyone to start cleaning up and keep cleaning up as part of their work routines (sometimes at the expense of production) is a big motivational exercise.

This is backed up by spending some money in the control room areas (the most important impact of productivity), which are usually the least cared-for areas. Often the most important people running the control room of the operation have the oldest chairs and the worst "hand me down" equipment like desks, fridges, ovens and kitchen facilities. What does this say about how important management feels about the heart of the operation?

Replacement of old furniture, fridges, microwaves, window treatments, and a fresh lick of paint often does the trick. Roads were cleaned, the plant was painted, new landscaping was done and general signage upgraded. Almost immediately there's a general sense of "let's be proud of our workplace".

My friend calls this the "toilet test". She says that using the toilet in any office, restaurant, or shop tells you a lot about the place. *"It was always the first thing I did when visiting a new client. Management could really benefit from using their workforce' toilets – it's a blinding flash of the obvious"*, she says.

It sends a very clear signal: when there's pride in your workplace, little things matter, working as a team matters, and performance matters. Over the longer period, productivity will usually improve dramatically in all areas.

Why does it work?
So why does simple housekeeping produce such a significant and extensive impact on general productivity? When I did it, I was essentially harnessing the Hawthorne effect. The Hawthorne effect is named after what was one of the most famous series of experiments in industrial history. The experiments took place at Western Electric's factory at Hawthorne, a suburb of Chicago, in the late 1920s and early 1930s. In these lighting experiments, light intensity was altered to examine its effect on worker productivity.

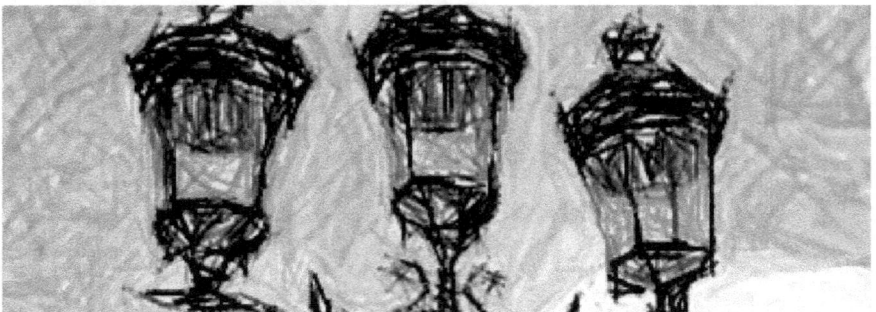

Results showed that productivity increased with higher illumination levels (after consultation with workforce) and surprisingly also increased when the lights were turned down (to the point of darkness). The researchers concluded that it was not the changes in physical conditions that were affecting the workers' productivity. Instead, it was the fact that someone was actually concerned about their workplace, and the opportunities this gave them to discuss changes before they happened.

Hawthorne established that the performance of employees is influenced by their surroundings and by the people they're working with as much as by their own innate abilities. In other experiments, other changes such as maintaining clean workstations, clearing floors of obstacles, and even relocating workstations resulted in increased productivity.

You as the reader might think I am being over simplistic by using such a basic tool as the Hawthorne effect. But I've found that backed with communication, passion for a happy, kind and compassionate culture, as well as employee motivation and 'belonging' produces real improvement in productivity.

Communication...
The second area is communication. Usually the reason the business or organisation is in such a poor state (so poor that a change manager has to be brought in) is that nobody knows what is going on, and over time, nobody cares what's going on anymore.

We check-in to work and check-out our mind and passion because it hurts too much to see and experience the workplace in that state. It's easier to detach from the political crap going on around you. It hurts too much to care and want to do something about it, so we leave our hearts and minds at home.

The first job of a change manager is to start engaging the workforce once again. There's a high degree of scepticism and you have to win them over with your vision, passion and energy. In the end, people have to like you before they follow you as a leader. It's not often expressed so bluntly but it is a realistic fact of leadership.

You need to inspire people to your cause. You are no different to a cult leader inspiring people to change their well-established behaviour and patterns. Constant, open, honest, transparent communication is the key to building this trust and inspiration.

Once every six months I implemented the "state of the nation" group briefings with the entire workforce, a monthly team brief system and weekly flat two-way communication structures. I discuss these tools in Chapter 4. These communication efforts re-engaged the workforce so that they began to care about their workplace once again.

In one of my favourite articles at the time 'When your culture needs a makeover' by Carol Berwick (company president of American corporation Alberto-Culver), I read the words: *"After a long history of management's keeping its cards close to the vest, we needed to open up and explain the business to our people. We wanted to create a world of in-your-face honesty and shared ownership of results".*

Berwick was able to turn her organisation around after a period of flat sales by getting every employee involved in making business decisions.

Other factors...

Of course, change management relies on the many factors that affect and influence workplace culture. These are all sufficiently covered in the previous chapters. In the end, after many years of passion, persistence and patience, we achieved turnaround results with this particular operation achieving record profits and a 30% improvement over the previous year.

Employees who believe that management is concerned about them as a whole person - not just an employee - are more productive, more satisfied, more fulfilled. Satisfied employees mean satisfied customers, which leads to profitability

Anne M Mulcahy

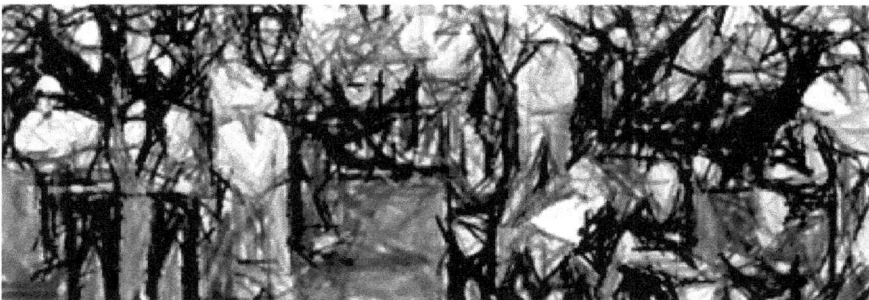

Change management...

In essence, change management is not easy and is often a vitality zapping exercise. It's for this reason I'd rather set up a workplace culture from scratch. That's why I build organisations (start-ups) from a handful of people to hundreds of people from the ground up. It is the workplace culture you establish as a small team and then allow to expand, maintaining the culture as it grows. Part of the way to do this is to make sure that people joining the organisation share the same passion about the importance of workplace culture.

In a nutshell...

Driving cultural change within an organisation is probably one of the hardest things to do as a manager. The two main things that will get the biggest bang for your buck on the cultural change front are in the areas of housekeeping and communication. It does sound deceptively simple, but it works.

Chapter 15
Time to get back to basics

Time to get back to basics

Employees are fatigued by the plethora of management initiatives that have surfaced over the decades. They're sick and tired of all the latest management philosophies and programs that they have had to endure. With every new initiative, there's the management speak that goes with it. Yes, sadly, I have been part of this machine as well.

Management jargon bingo...

Even as a manager within a large executive management team, our favourite game was buzzword bingo. In case you're not familiar with the game, it's just like bingo but you pick a set of management jargon words that are likely to come up at a meeting. Pick say five words or phrases: "paradigm shift", "empowerment", "low-hanging fruit", "bandwidth" and "alignment". As the meeting progresses, you tick them off as some corporate manager utters one of them. The winner is first to hit all five words. It's not recommended that you shout "BINGO" during the meeting but quietly mouthing it to the rest of the players is satisfactory.

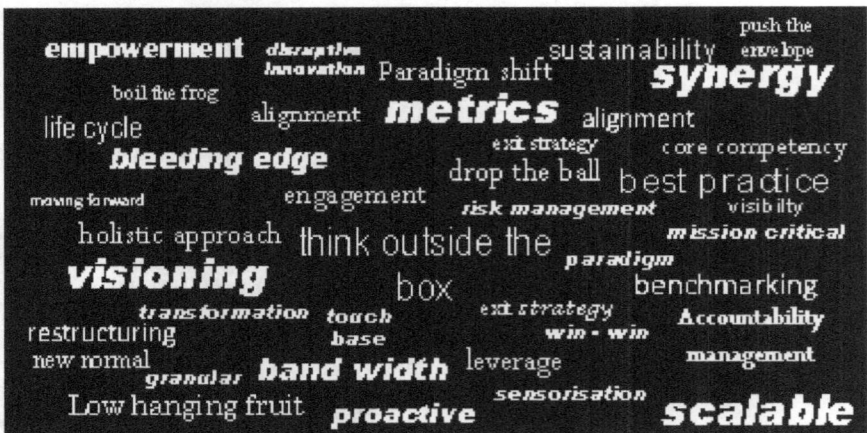

I once had a boss who loved using *"zero sum game" and "above board"*. These were always a sure bet on my bingo card. Unfortunately, as executive managers, that's what we thought about the corporate game we were participating in. The whole system of management-speak and corporate jargon is ridiculous. Some believe management speak is typically used to make something seem more impressive than it actually is. Others believe management speak is designed to intimidate or confuse employees.

Now if that's what we thought as managers, what about the people in the organisation and on the shop floor? Of course, they've always thought this management jargon is a lot of bull and it drives them mad. Can you think of some of your own pet-hates when it comes to this kind of language?

In a recent article from The Telegraph, it was reported that this kind of jargon is used in two thirds of offices across Britain and that nearly a quarter of workers consider it to be a *"pointless irritation"*. More than just an annoyance, the overused phrases can hold back business and leave workers feeling isolated.

"Thinking outside the box" – meaning to look at things differently – was voted the most annoying overused term, followed by the phrase *"going forward"* – meaning in the future – and then *"let's touch base"* – used when the person wants to call, email or meet to discuss an issue.

Chrissie Mahler, founder of the Plain English Campaign, said that there is a serious side to the irritation and overused jargon that could be holding British businesses back. *"Management speak gets in the way...instead of sitting in the office irritated by jargon, people need to stand up and tell their bosses that they are not making any sense,"* Mahler explains.

Last year, a survey revealed that people working in big corporate organisations found themselves using management speak as a way of disguising the fact that they hadn't done their job properly. Some people think it's easy to bluff their way through by using long, impressive-sounding words and phrases, even if they don't know what they mean.

Our business is infested with idiots who try to impress by using pretentious jargon.

David Ogilvy

Getting back to the basics...

As we push towards modern management and technology, we're constantly forced to move away from basic, face-to-face management of our people. We've overcomplicated management practices. Getting back to basics relates to the principle that most systems work best if they are kept simple rather than made complicated by management. Simplicity should be a key goal in the way we manage our people.

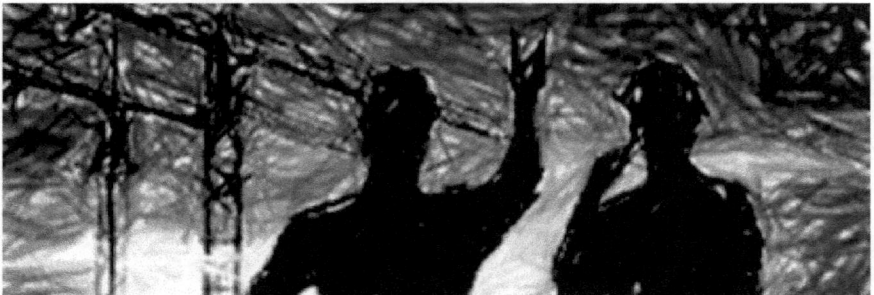

The requirements of a supervisor or manager have become more onerous. These people have to be computer savvy, have good communication, administration skills, coaching and mentoring skills, be adaptable to change, disciplined, approachable and hands-on.

Typically, during the early part of my career, supervisors were selected and promoted due mainly to their people management abilities and skills. They were great leaders, well respected and great at handling people. I remember two of my "bosses" back then in the chemical industry made their way up the management ranks.

One was originally an operator and one was a laboratory technician. You didn't necessary have to have a university degree to be a manager. They were great managers to watch and learn your trade from. Unfortunately, due to the pressure and requirements of being a modern manager, the skill and art of managing and dealing with people is rated less today. Where is the EQ criteria when we recruit managers?

Let's strip back the complicated systems that have taken our managers and supervisors away from basic people management. Let's stop wasting our precious time and resources measuring and evaluating and instead allow and trust our managers to do their job. If you believe you have the right people, then give them the freedom, the authority, the delegation to innovate, perform and lead.

> *Most of what we call management consists of making*
> *it difficult for people to get their work done.*
>
> Peter Drucker

In a nutshell...

Employees are sick and tired with the plethora of management initiatives that have surfaced over the decades. They want basic, face-to-face people management. Much of the reoccurring theme in this book is the need to strip back the overcomplicated systems that have taken our managers and supervisors away from basic people management. If you believe you have the right people, then give them the freedom, the authority, the delegation to innovate, perform and lead.

Chapter 16
It's a wrap

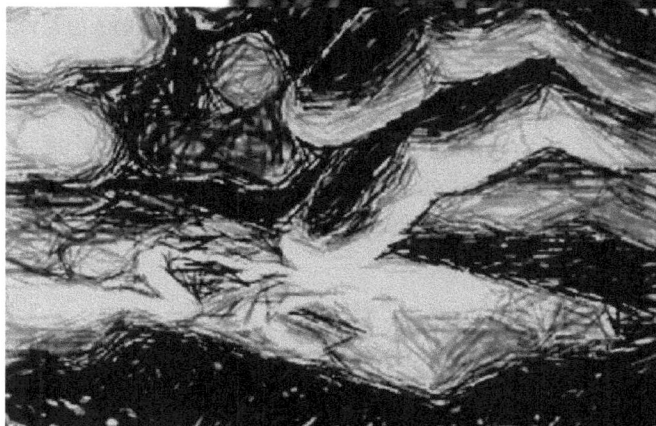

It's a wrap

Over my years of management experience and study of management, I've come to believe that we can develop some alternative views and techniques for managing people better. Our objective is always to create happy, kind, dynamic and highly-effective organisations with a social conscience.

> **Employee comments:**
> *"The way that Iggy, as a CEO, tirelessly works to ensure that a team-based culture prevails in the organisations that he leads, is in my experience quite unique. He truly has provided the most inclusive and rewarding work environment of my professional career. Although this book provides an overview of how and why he is able to achieve this – it understates the discipline and effort required of the CEO to actually make it happen."*
>
> Shane Volk (CFO)
> Current employee

It doesn't really matter what anyone writes in corporate value statements. The true values of an organisation's culture comes from "the way we do things around here". The most important of these behaviours is the direct behaviour of the CEO or leader/s of the organisation. There is often a huge difference between an organisation's published values and the actual behaviour of the organisation, which causes a disconnection and distrust within the workplace.

Unfortunately, the majority of employees believe that performance appraisals are a waste of time, of little benefit, and demoralising. In fact, the appraisal can create so much frustration and angst in employees that it becomes counterproductive for improving performance. The performance appraisal system and our reward system for individual performance has accidentally created a competitive, "looking good" and "blame" workplace culture. Ban the performance appraisal and instead reward team performance, which in turn will create a workplace culture where informal, regular, timely and immediate

———————●———————

In order to achieve effective teamwork, we need to change the reward system and encourage employees to help each other to achieve the overall team targets. Compensation, bonuses, and rewards must depend on collaborative practices rather than individual contribution and achievement. Teamwork is about embracing the differences in people. The fabric and types of people that make up a team reflect society and the sooner we can all embrace the concept that we can't all be high-flyers the better. Set global targets and if they are achieved then everyone in the entire team gets rewarded equally. People generally want to work in these caring, compassionate and happy workplaces.

———————●———————

Constant, open, honest, and transparent communication is hard work and the benefits and results are not often immediately obvious. In my simplistic view, that hard work is essential in creating the feeling of connectedness that binds people within a group or organisation. We need that web of connectedness in order to become a high-performing organisation.

———————●———————

Setting individual objectives or key performance indicators, monitoring them and evaluating them, is a waste of time and resources. The KPI system serves little purpose except to drive a competitive environment and discourage a culture of teamwork. Why implement a system that encourages competition by trying to "look good"? What motivates people is people.

———○———

Job descriptions have become blueprints for silos. We have accidentally created a workplace culture that discourages our employees to go beyond their roles, co-operate and help one another. We need to create organisations in which it becomes individually useful for people to co-operate and where they are rewarded for doing so.

———○———

The traditional exit interview for employee resignations is a waste of time and way too late. Exit interviews are a retrospective management tool rather than a proactive forward-looking indicator of the health of the organisation. The questions are, however, very important and should be directed to employees before they resign from the organisation. It is also important for organisations to acknowledge the value and loyal service of departing employees and ensuring a proper farewell as they are the future ambassadors of your organisation.

———○———

Gauge the health of your organisation by using employee surveys on a regular basis to measure employee engagement, morale and performance. Openly share the results with every employee and let the teams sort it out for themselves. When you have motivated and engaged employees, whilst trusting the process, we find that over time, these results improve.

———○———

Mission statements serve no purpose whatsoever and are of little benefit. They all look and sound like they have been written by a mass mission-statement generator. On the other hand, a vision is a forward-looking and action-based statement. It gathers the momentum of the organisation. A simple but powerful vision unifies the organisation's common purpose and direction. It is very important to have a vision as it is the backbone of workplace culture enabling it to evolve over time.

A 'no blame' culture is essential for an organisation to make decisions without fear. The underlying philosophy is that there is no such thing as a right or wrong decision. The organisation recognises that not all the information is needed at the time but any decision is more important than no decision. Innate intuition is encouraged. Risk management is highly important in the decision-making process. This hopefully nurtures an organisation where fast, dynamic, high-quality, fearless decision-making and execution are the norm.

The recruitment policy should not be to find the "best person for the job". While finding someone who can do the job is a requirement, most importantly, we find someone who fits into the workplace culture the best. Someone who contributes to the workplace harmony and the productivity of the team environment. By throwing away the CV at the interview stage we can focus and rely solely on other clues, our innate intuition or gut feeling as part of the selection process.

Dismissing employees is difficult for the employee as well as the organisation. The way we dismiss employees should be exactly the same way that you would like to be dismissed yourself; hopefully with some respect and dignity and the acknowledgment of the valuable loyalty and service you've provided.

Basic positive thinking and acting in a positive manner within the workplace will create a healthier, happier and more effective working environment. The behaviour of acting in a positive manner affects the culture and overall morale. Organisations must strive to focus on doing the right things rather than doing things right and in the process, simplify the business and cut-out the office politics.

Reinforcing the standard principle of always thinking "two steps ahead" and taking those actions ahead of time creates a very proactive, energetic workplace culture. The benefit is a management group that is calm, in control and happy, particularly when faced with negative issues. Visualisation of successes is a powerful way for leaders in an organisation to program their subconscious mind, set the intentional energy, positive energy and tap into the power of self-fulfilling prophesy to achieve the organisation's goals.

Driving cultural change within an organisation is probably one of the hardest things to do as a manager. The two main things that will get the biggest bang for your buck on the cultural change front are in the areas of housekeeping – the pulse of morale, efficiency and the health of a business; and communication – open, honest, transparent to engage and inspire. It does sound deceptively simple, but it works.

Employees are sick and tired with the plethora of management initiatives that have surfaced over the decades. They want basic, face-to-face people management and leadership.

Much of the reoccurring theme in this book is the need to strip back the overcomplicated systems that have taken our managers and supervisors away from basic people management. If you believe you have the right people, then give them the freedom, the authority, the delegation to innovate, perform and lead.

Final Acknowledgement

In memory of
Gang Liu and Xiaochun Yuan